FURNITURE BY ARCHITECTS

FURNITURE BY ARCHITECTS

International Masterpieces of Twentieth-Century Design and Where to Buy Them

Expanded Edition

by Marc Emery

Harry N. Abrams, Inc., Publishers, New York

TO VICA AND AURÈLE

On preceding pages:

Angelo Mangiarotti. *Incas*. Table in La Versilia marble. Manufacturer: Fucina/Skipper

Le Corbusier. *LC 7*. Revolving armchair in chrome-plated or colored enamel steel frame with back and seat cushions. 1925–28. Manufacturer: Cassina

Gaetano Pesce. *Dalila Uno, Due, Tre*. Chairs in molded hard polyurethane. 1980. Manufacturer: Cassina

Alvar Aalto. Armchair in wood and plywood. 1930–33. Manufacturer: Artek

On these pages:

Angelo Mangiarotti. *Alola*. Floor lamps with adjustable reflectors. Manufacturer: Pollux/Skipper

For the original edition:
Project Director: Margaret L. Kaplan
Editor: Anne Yarowsky
Designer: Patrick Cunningham

For the expanded edition:
Editor: Margaret Blythe Rennolds
Designer: Gilda Hannah

Library of Congress Cataloging in Publication Data
Emery, Marc.
   Furniture by architects.
   Includes index.
1. Furniture design. 2. Architects
3. Furniture—Catalogs. I. Title.
TT196.E48 1983   749.2'049'0294   83–2581
ISBN 0–8109–0902–2

CONTENTS

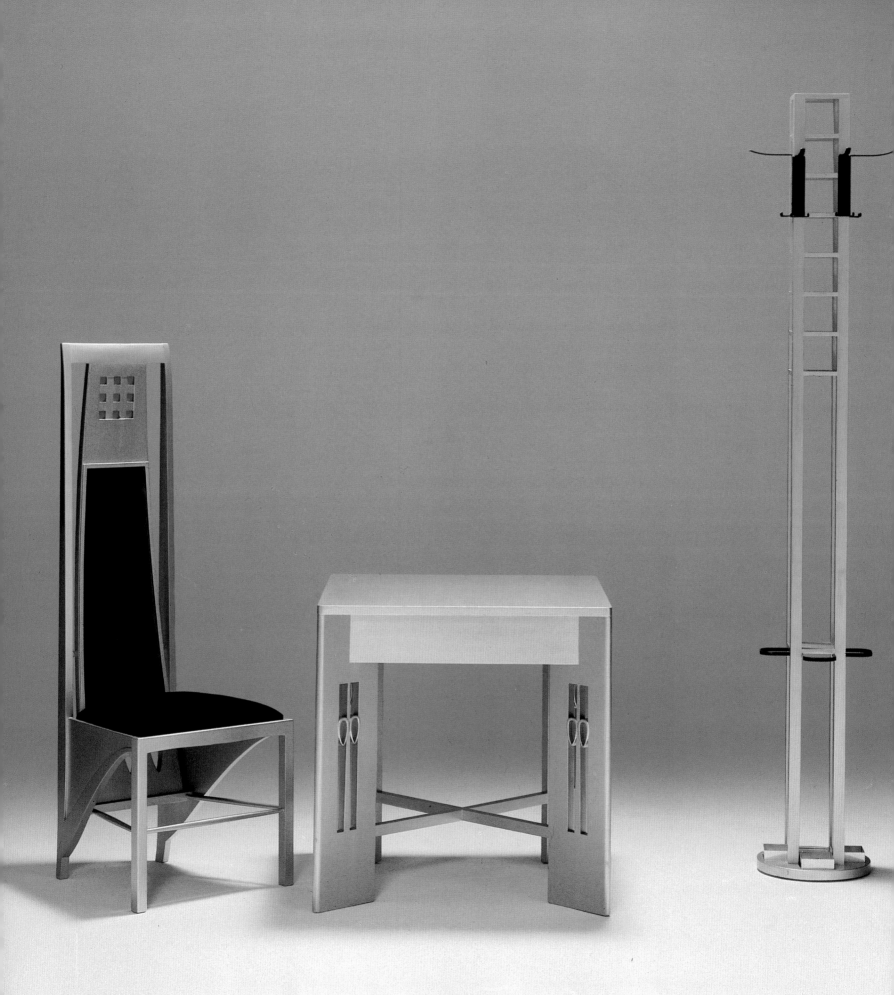

INTRODUCTION

This furniture had the elegance and wit for which his architecture was already remarkable.
—*J. M. Richards, 1977*

Opposite: Charles Rennie Mackintosh. Chair in silver-painted oak, 1903; square table in silver-painted wood, 1903; coat and umbrella stand in silver-painted mahogany. Manufacturer: B.D. Ediciones

Following: Marcel Breuer. *Cesca* armchair, 1928; *Cesca* armless chair, 1928; *Laccio* table, 1925; *Wassily* lounge chair, 1925; reclining chair, 1925. Manufacturer: Knoll International

The architect as total designer, the person who designs and controls every aspect in the creation of a building, seems to be a half-forgotten concept today, although it was a common practice in the eighteenth and nineteenth centuries and likely in the Middle Ages. It was not, however, before the Arts and Crafts movement—a puritan reaction against the vulgarity of mass-produced objects and the ornamental excesses of the Victorian era—that the architect's comprehensive role in the decorative and domestic arts was fully achieved. Architectural practices then were normally perceived as the conception of a building as well as the decoration and design of objects that would furnish it. The Arts and Crafts architects were soon to be followed by a whole generation of young architects anxious to prove their professional abilities in the areas of interior and furniture design: among them Guimard in Paris, Gaudí in Barcelona, Mackintosh in Glasgow, Wright in Chicago, and Hoffmann in Vienna.

For most of these architects, the furniture they designed was created with the whole of the specific site in mind; they could not conceive of the furniture used elsewhere. But Josef Hoffmann thought differently and launched a business venture, the Wiener Werkstätte, where he produced and commercialized his own furniture and later the furniture of his colleagues. Commercialization of good modern furniture was then a common practice, but commercialization of furniture designed by architects was an important new step that not only limited the architect's control over how and where his furniture would be used, but that promoted the architect into the new role of industrial designer.

The architect's changing role was accompanied by a new kind of architectural practice. The expansion of pre- and postwar industrialization forced architects to face the fact that they could not sustain an upperclass practice dealing with upperclass clients. Soon they would be mobilized to solve other types of problems, namely that of mass-housing. To meet this challenge they set themselves up as total designers, capable of solving any and all questions in their field through the application of their own logic. Domestic furniture design became an architectural problem similar to others: The furniture would be mass-produced and made from modern industrial materials—aluminum, steel, bent plywood, glass, or Plexiglas—and it would be inexpensive, hence available to the middle- and lower-middle-classes. The Breuer chair (1928) is typical of the time. It was easy to build (bent steel tubing), easy to

11

clean, rather comfortable, and its modular aesthetic expressed the industrial world that produced it.

In retrospect, the industrial aesthetic demonstrated in the Breuer chair seems to have been a major concern among designers of the period. Was its achievement a reaction against the delicate plainness pursued by the Arts and Crafts movement, or against the decadent curves of Art Nouveau? Or, more likely, was it due to a blind faith in the brave new world just around the corner? Perhaps it was the expression of a bitter, secret resentment against the industrial world itself, the success of which was so impressive that the only way for architects to recover some of its power was to copy its forms.

Ironically, the furniture designed by architects advocating mass production and its resulting inexpensiveness often turned out to be luxury items. The Red and Blue Chair Gerrit Rietveld designed and built with his own hands in 1918 was not only an aesthetic manifesto, but a clear demonstration that a piece of furniture could be so simple in its conception that its production could easily be industrialized. Unfortunately, this was not the case, and for many years the Red and Blue Chair was not mass-produced. Now that it is, it has become something of an art object rather than a functional piece of furniture. The Breuer chair, however, has not fallen into this category. Today it is mass-produced and functions comfortably as a chair.

In the 1940s and 1950s, the concept of the architect as total designer, or more accurately, as a furniture designer, took various forms in Europe and America. It was, and still is, a common practice in Denmark, where formal boundaries between architectural and industrial design were never drawn and where architects designed furniture as a natural complement to their projects. For a long time architectural training in Denmark was based on an artistic, or craftsman-oriented, superstructure, and the architect felt like an artisan. In Danish, the word architect means "supreme carpenter."

The preeminent Danish architect Arne Jacobsen was internationally recognized as an industrial designer. His work encompassed, on the one hand, curtain-walled buildings, row houses, and embassies, and, on the other, armchairs, office furniture, and plumbing features. Jacobsen's diverse practice was maintained by his successors, Hans Dissing and

Otto Weitling, who undertook the renewal of the Copenhagen Central Station while completing the Danish National Bank simultaneously. One of Dissing and Weitling's most recent projects has been the design of bifocal glasses. Other Danish architects—among them Poul Kjaerholm, Hans Wegner, Verner Panton—have shown more interest in furniture design than in building design and have gained international reputations.

In Italy the situation is similar, although modern Italian architects have been less involved with craftsmanship and more interested in industrial design. The late Italian architect Ernesto Rogers once claimed that "the field of architecture covers everything from teaspoon design to urban planning" and demonstrated this by designing the kinds of things his Italian colleagues did—cutlery, lamps, monuments, schools, urban renewal projects, skyscrapers, housing, shops, chairs, ceramics, and espresso machines. Another well-known Italian architect of this period, Gio Ponti, was editor of the influential design magazine *Domus* while he designed skyscrapers and cars. Today Gae Aulenti, Vittorio Gregotti, and Paolo Portoghesi, among other famous Italian architects, practice this concept of total design. Gae Aulenti is perhaps better known as an industrial designer, yet she maintains a solid architectural practice. Gregotti, famous for his studies on the relationship between man and his territories, is presently building two provincial universities while he designs lamps,

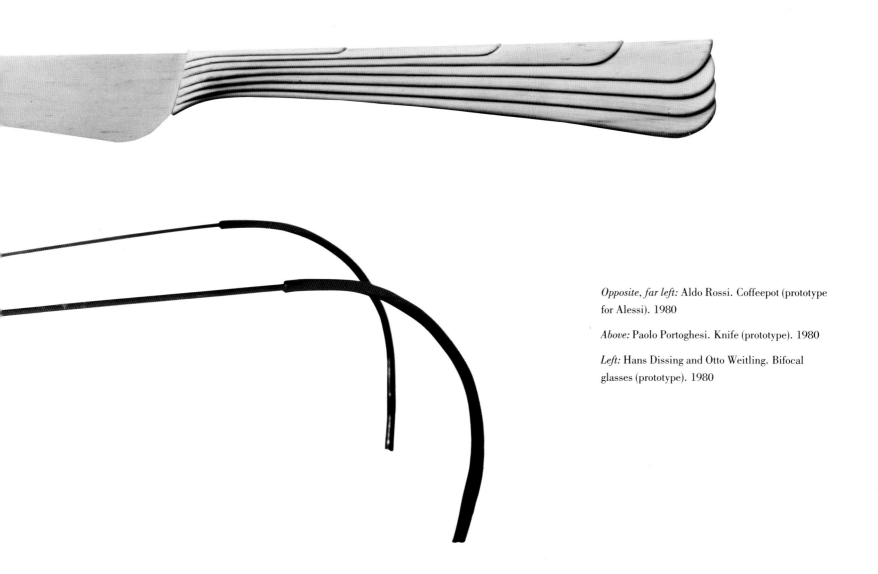

Opposite, far left: Aldo Rossi. Coffeepot (prototype for Alessi). 1980

Above: Paolo Portoghesi. Knife (prototype). 1980

Left: Hans Dissing and Otto Weitling. Bifocal glasses (prototype). 1980

armchairs, and elegant fashion shops in Milan. Like architects in Denmark, some Italian architects have been more inclined toward industrial design rather than architecture. Among the stars of contemporary Italian industrial and furniture design, many were trained and practiced as architects.

For reasons that could be cultural, most other European architects have shown more interest in architectural projects and building than in sidefields such as furniture. Perhaps this is because many countries have kept the two practices of architecture and interior/furniture design segregated. Germany, for example—a country where many pioneers of modern design were architects—seems to have made such a distinction, although many of the German designers were trained at the Ulm Hochschule für Gestaltung, a postwar revival of the Bauhaus. The same could be said of the Netherlands and of Britain, where the shadows of Mackintosh and Rietveld were unable to sustain practices.

Spain and Portugal have long witnessed academically conservative practices in architectural training, and except for Barcelona and Porto, there has been no working philosophy of the architect as total designer. In Barcelona, architects have always considered the various aspects of their practice from a total design standpoint, the way Gaudí used to do; but Gaudí was probably practicing the way his own contemporaries did—designing among other useful and ingenious items, small furniture, house appliances, objects, and outdoor furniture. In Porto, Alvaro Siza often designs his clients' furniture and local craftsmen sometimes produce it in small editions.

In the United States, the dual practices of building and furniture design have been well anchored in architects' habits since the days of Jefferson. Those carrying on the tradition have included Frank Furness, Henry Hobson Richardson, Frank Lloyd Wright, the Greene brothers, Bernard Maybeck, Rudolf Schindler, Eero Saarinen, Charles Eames, and Michael Graves. Like the Europeans, the American architects have designed comprehensive interiors with furniture, but unlike the Europeans, the interiors have sometimes been designed for office buildings, and large quantities of specific office furniture have been produced. Such was the case with the Larkin Building (destroyed in 1950) in Buffalo, New York, and the Johnson Wax headquarters in Racine, Wisconsin, both designed by Frank Lloyd Wright.

Architects figured prominently in the golden age of American design, an era that began in 1940, when Charles Eames and Eero Saarinen won the "Organic Design in Home Furnishing" competition organized by The Museum of Modern Art in New York. The idea behind the competition was to promote modern design rather than the various pseudo-styles then dominating the American furniture market.

Most of the entries in the competition were designs with good aesthetic and technical qualities, but Eames and Saarinen's proposal was unique. Their chair was made of bent plywood molded in two directions. This was a strikingly new idea, one that had gone a step further than other designers had carried it up to that time. The step was prophetic, for it announced the future implications of advanced technologies in the furniture industry and the as yet unknown possibilities of plastic. The Eames/Saarinen winning entry also possessed, in potentiality, the criteria that would characterize contemporary furniture design: wholeness,

Antonio Gaudí. *Battló Bench*. Bench in American oak. 1905–7. Manufacturer: B.D. Ediciones

Opposite: Gae Aulenti. *Melograno*. Lounge chair, settee, sofa, and coffee table. Manufacturer: Knoll International

Above: Eero Saarinen. Settee, 1948; easy chair (Womb chair), 1948; and ottoman, 1950. Manufacturer: Knoll International

Below: Eero Saarinen. Armchairs, 1956; side chair, 1956; stool, 1956; and tables, 1956. Manufacturer: Knoll International

beauty, comfort, modern materials, modern technologies, and strength.

Charles Eames continued his experiments with molded plywood and received a commission from the United States Navy to produce molded plywood stretchers and splints. In 1946 he began to produce a molded plywood chair whose production was later taken over by the American firm Herman Miller.

The person responsible for bringing Eames to Herman Miller—a collaboration that lasted until Eames's death—was another young modern architect, George Nelson, who was then design director for the company. Nelson had caught the attention of this Midwest firm through his designing of a storage wall unit, an innovation that revolutionized home storage techniques in the mid-1940s.

Competing with Herman Miller and the other firms that produced modern furniture was the small but innovative and ambitious firm Knoll, a company that had been created by a young German immigrant and his American wife. In less than a decade, Knoll turned into a furniture design empire. The success of Hans and Florence Knoll—passionate believers in the idea that modern architecture needed modern furniture—lay not only in their talent to select good unknown designers, but also in their American reproduction of Mies van der Rohe and Marcel Breuer's European furniture, a practice that promoted top-quality design in America.

Having established connections with the firm early on, Eero Saarinen designed a chair for Knoll in laminated wood. It was a good piece of furniture, but it did not sell successfully. His breakthrough came later, in 1948, first with his "Womb" chair—a fiberglass molded shell with metallic legs—and next with his No. 71—a fiberglass chair chosen to furnish the General Motors Technical Center in Warren, Michigan. The No. 71 chair perfectly matched the modern classicism of this twentieth-century Versailles and definitively established him as a leading architect.

Unlike many other architect/furniture designers, Saarinen's approach to his buildings was different from his approach to furniture design: "Though we use mass-produced parts in architecture," he wrote in 1957, "a building is custom-built to the extent it is a solution of a

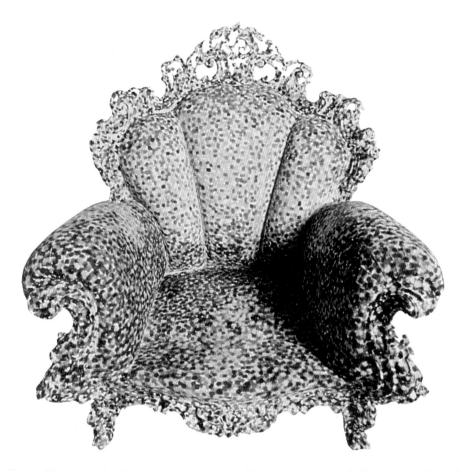

specific problem. . . . In furniture design, the client is every man." Saarinen believed that mass-produced furniture must fit into a wide variety of unknown contexts and that therefore a well-designed piece of furniture, like an art object, must be able to impose itself into whatever the context is; like art it must have wholeness.

The Womb chair was Saarinen's attempt to answer these modern needs. In designing it he remarked that "people sit differently today than in the Victorian era." For him such a chair could be used in many ways since "a comfortable position, even if it were the most comfortable in the world, would not be so for very long." Moreover, "the chair should not only look well as a piece of sculpture in the room when no one is in it, it should also be a flattering background when someone is in it, especially the female occupant." The Womb chair became such an American success that it appeared in a Norman Rockwell cover of the *Saturday Evening Post*.

Although Saarinen enjoyed the success of the Womb chair, he was not altogether pleased with its design. The chair had four legs, and Saarinen did not like the "slum of legs." "One piece, one material" seemed to be his motto, when, in the late 1950s, he designed the Tulip chair made of molded plastic balanced on a stem aluminum pedestal. The Tulip chair was a bold structural step, a demonstration that a plastic shell supported by an aluminum one-leg base was no longer a utopian concept but one based in reality. Reality it was. The chair is a technical achievement, a sculptural and elegant object, and a comfortable piece of furniture.

Like Saarinen, Eames had been intrigued by comfort and its new forms. However, his own solutions to the problem differed sharply from those of Saarinen. His famous lounge chair from the mid-1950s cannot be considered an answer to the Womb chair but another way to answer an already solved problem. Made of laminated rosewood "petals" padded with leather cushions and joined with aluminum connections, the chair was mounted on a metal swivel base.

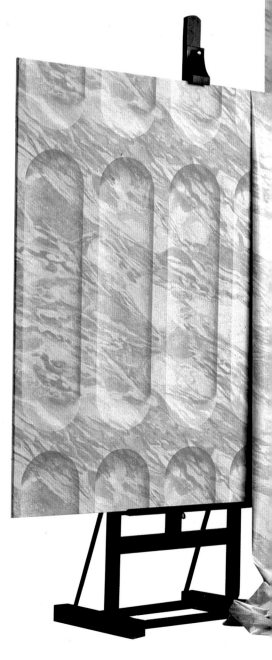

Opposite: Alessandro Mendini. *Armchair for Proust*. 1979. Collection "Bau.haus, side one." Manufacturer: Studio Alchymia

Below: Trix and Robert Haussmann and Alfred Hablutzel. Fabric. Manufacturer: Mira-X

Over twenty-five years later Eames's chair has become a timeless classic, but during those twenty-five years the field has changed drastically. The outbreak of the so-called economic crisis in the early 1970s produced radical effects on the architectural scene. It not only reduced the architect's workload and commissions, but it provoked an intellectual crisis. Functionalism, which through its American achievements had become a sort of official credo, could not be trusted anymore. It had been challenged first by the Philadelphia architect Louis Kahn and later by another Philadelphian, Robert Venturi. For his part Kahn questioned a modern architecture whose practices he considered mere religious rituals, while Venturi showed, through an essay published in 1967, that architecture was an art with many parameters, and that most of those parameters had been overshadowed, if not caricaturized, by the modern masters. Both men demonstrated that the cultural roots of contemporary architecture were not contained in the "technicalities" of the modern movement. For Venturi, the dictatorship of modernism had prevented the expression of other aesthetic values such as those of contemporary mass-culture praised by the Pop artists.

Largely inspired by Kahn and Venturi, a new wave of movements, trends, and polemics arose that sparked interest in architectural pre-modern history. Suddenly architects began to rediscover the nineteenth-century masters' works and writings and found that many of these men's theories were far from obsolete. A vogue of formal historicism, or historic formalism, developed rapidly: It was Post-Modernism.

The questioning of modern architecture changed the furniture industry in two significant ways: first, it generated a new demand for antique modern furniture and second, it helped to create a new breed of "Post-Modern" furniture in which modern design rules were systematically rejected. Spurred by the interest in modern antiques, a vogue for furniture re-editions followed. Most of these re-editions were based on furniture designed by architects. Some of the new "Post-Modern" furniture derives from the reinterpretation of these re-editions through formal distortion, stylistic copies, caricature. Its influence is currently felt throughout the furniture industry, even among prominent conservative designers, but if "Joke furniture" may look funny, it will probably never constitute a sound response to specific needs the way modern furniture did.

The future of furniture design—with or without architects—is not in short-term jokes or in the restyling of modern antiques; it is in something else that implies the experience of modern design and the tremendous advances of technologies that have gone far beyond what it was twenty years ago. What its forms, shapes, logic, and techniques will be are pending questions, and in their own way are the reasons for this book.

Architects were not the only interior or furniture designers of their times. They were not even the best. They were, however, among the few—due to their position—who understood, perhaps more than other artists, that the forces of mass production, functionalism, technology, changes in living habits, and social movements would profoundly alter modern society, and with this knowledge they expressed these feelings. Architecture was one mode of that expression; furniture design another, and, as it may be seen in this book, it was not the worst.

M.E.

Alvar Aalto

Franco Albini and Franca Helg

ARCHIZOOM

Gae Aulenti

Note:

Information for the furniture shown has been given when available from the manufacturers' catalogues. The manufacturer is indicated at the end of each caption, the address of which can be found in the Index. Unless otherwise specified, the order of the dimensions is given width by depth by height. Dates for objects refer to the year of their design.

Alvar Aalto (1898–1976)

One of the most famous masters of the modern movement, Alvar Aalto was born in Finland, a country of little resources and wild, natural land. Strongly influenced by the Finnish terrain, Aalto developed a highly personal approach to architecture that combined natural materials and lights. His organic but extremely elegant structures soon won international acclaim, among them the Tuberculosis Sanatorium in Paimio, Finland; the Town Hall in Säynätsalo, Finland; and the Baker House Dormitory at the Massachusetts Institute of Technology.

Aalto's thoughtful care for detail led him to design furniture he considered natural complements to his buildings. Using Finnish birchwood and the most advanced techniques of the time (bent laminated wood) he conceived, first for his sanatorium in Paimio and then for his library in Viipuri (now part of Russia), a set of tables, chairs, and armchairs, which, now classics of modern furniture, were produced by Artek, a firm he formed with his wife, Aino, and his lifelong patron, Mairea Gullichsøn.

1. Armchair. 1930–33. Wood and plywood. 23⅜ x 31¼ x 24⅞". Artek
2. Stackable row chair. 1930. Birch; seat and back in plywood or upholstered. 19 x 19¼ x 31½". Artek
3. Stackable armchair. 1931–33. Seat and back in bent plywood. 21 x 24½ x 30⅝". Artek
4. Armchair. 1933. Laminated wood with upholstered seat and back. 24 x 27½ x 28½". Artek
5. Drawer unit. 1930. Birch. Each unit 15 x 21⅝ x 25⅝". Artek
6. Armchair. 1933. Laminated wood with upholstered seat and back. 24⅝ x 31½ x 39¼". Artek
7. Round table. 1933. Wood. Diameter 39½"; height 28". Artek
8. Table. 1933. Wood. 39½ x 23⅝ x 28". Artek
9. Table. Wood. 85⅞ x 46¾ x 27⅝". Artek
10. Table. Wood. Small table 28½ x 15¾ x 17¼"; large table 44 x 15¾ x 17¼". Artek
11. Stackable stool. 1933. Wood. Diameter 13¼"; height 17¼". Artek
12. Stool. Birch. Diameter 20¼"; height 25⅝". Artek
13. Stackable chair. 1933–35. Birch; back laminated, legs solid wood. 15 x 19 x 26½". Artek
14. Chair. Birch. 15⅝ x 19 x 29⅛". Artek
15. Chair. 1933–35. Back in bent plywood. 15 x 16½ x 30¼". Artek
16. Chair. 1933–35. Back in bent plywood. 13¾ x 15 x 26". Artek
17. High chair. 1933–35. Back in bent plywood. 14 x 15 x 27¼". Artek
18. Tea trolley. 1936. Bent laminated frame; shelves with linoleum. 35½ x 19¾ x 22¼". Artek
19. Tea trolley. 1936. Bent laminated frame; shelves with linoleum. 35½ x 25½ x 23⅝". Artek
20. Armchair. 1936. Seat and back upholstered; supporting cantilevered side parts bent and laminated. 21½ x 30 x 23⅝". Artek
21. Easy chair. 1937. Laminated frame supporting cantilevered side parts bent and laminated; webbed covering. Artek
22. Shelves. 1936. Consoles laminated and bent into a closed curve. 39⅜ x 10⅝ x 10". Artek
23. Shelf. Console laminated and bent into closed curve. 39 x 10½ x 9¾". Artek
24. Table. 1947. Laminated and bent wooden legs; removable glass top. 27¼ x 27¼ x 17¼". Artek
25. Armchair. 1947. Supporting sides and frame laminated and bent; seat and back webbed or quilted. 24 x 23⅝ x 31½". Artek
26. Armchair. 1947. Supporting sides and frame laminated and bent; seat and back upholstered. 23⅝ x 25⅝ x 29¼". Artek
27. Armchair. 1947. Supporting sides and frame laminated and bent; seat and back upholstered. 24 x 23⅝ x 31½". Artek
28. Armchair. 1947. Supported cantilevered side parts laminated and bent; laminated seat frame webbed or quilted. 23⅝ x 28 x 32¾". Artek
29. Stool. 1954. Round seat ash-veneered or upholstered. 15 x 15 x 17¾". Artek
30. Stool. 1954. Square-shaped seat ash-veneered or upholstered. 17¾ x 17¾ x 17¾". Artek
31. Table. 1954. Top ash- or oak-veneered. 35½ x 35½ x 22". Artek
32. Table. 1954–56. Straight legs of solid wood. 51¼ x 35½ x 28¾". Artek
33. Table. 1954–56. Straight legs of solid wood. 58⅛ x 31½ x 27½". Artek
34. Bed. Legs of laminated and bent wood. 80 x 36 x 13¾". Artek
35. Cabinet. Wood. 35½ x 17¾ x 25⅝". Artek
36. Cabinet with drawers. Wood. 35½ x 17¾ x 22". Artek
37. *Aalto Sofa Bed.* Convertible sofa bed. 1930. Chromium-plated tubular steel with steel spring frame mattress; armrest in beech. Sofa 79½ x 33 x 27½"; bed 79½ x 35½ x 27½". ICF (U.S.)
38. Stool. 1947. Legs laminated and bent; seat webbed or quilted. 16⅛ x 16⅛ x 17¼". Artek

39. Hanging fixture. Brass; 60-watt bulb. Diameter 5"; height 7". Artek
40. Hanging fixture. Painted white with decorative brass brim; 100-watt bulb. Diameter 12½"; height 11⅜". Artek
41. Hanging fixture. White-painted aluminum or brass with inside painted white; 75-watt bulb. Diameter 11¾"; height 16⅜". Artek
42. Hanging fixture. Painted aluminum; 100-watt bulb. Diameter 23". Artek
43. Ceiling fixture. White-painted iron; 100-watt bulb. Diameter 23". Artek
44. Floor lamp. Globe with painted iron; foot covered with black leather; 150-watt bulb. Diameter 11¾"; height 67½". Artek
45. Floor lamp. Globe in iron, painted white; foot covered with black leather; three 75-watt bulbs. Height 65⅛". Artek
46. Flower vases. 1937. Glass. Artek
47. *Aalto*. Flower vases. 1936. Glass. Height 8½"; 14". Ittala Glassworks
48. *Aalto*. Flower vases. 1937. Glass. Height 4⅝". Ittala Glassworks

Franco Albini (1905–1977)
Franca Helg

One of the most outstanding architects of exhibitions and displays, the Italian-born Franco Albini radically influenced the face of museum design. His interior remodeling of the Renaissance museums—the Palazzo Rosso and the Palazzo Bianco—and his designing of the Treasury of S. Lorenzo, all in Genoa, are considered masterpieces of museum exhibition technique. With his partner, Franca Helg, Albini designed the most famous of their achievements, the Roman department store La Rinascente, a building with an exposed steel frame and windowless concrete walls.

49. *Ambra*. Door handle. Anodized aluminum, silver, or bronze. 4". Window handles also available. Olivari
50. Desk. Clear plate-glass top; squared steel tubing, chrome-plated base. 48 x 26 x 27½". Knoll International

ARCHIZOOM

Archizoom Associati, based in Florence, has been practicing as a group since 1966. In addition to their architectural projects they have organized several exhibitions and once published an issue of the Italian magazine In *devoted to the theme "Destruction of the Object."*

51. *Aeo* (P. Deganello). Chair (with or without arms). 1973. Gray durethan base; lacquered steel frame available in white or gray; foam polyurethane and Dacron padding; fabric or leather upholstery. 30⅞ x 27¼ x 41¾". Cassina

Gae Aulenti (b. 1927)

The Italian architect and professor Gae Aulenti is perhaps best known for her designs of furniture and objects. Personal concepts regarding architecture, cities, and the place and role of objects in modern societies have led her to controversial positions regarding industrial objects and their production. She has written: "The process of design can only find its proper relationship in a field of which it constitutes the center." According to Aulenti, objects must be considered in the framework of a global and complex environment.

52. *Melograno Acerbo*. Convertible armchair. Double-face lining; matching pillows and quilt blanket. 82⅝ x 44⅞ x 37⅛". Casa Nova
53. *Melograno*. Convertible sofa. Double-face lining; matching pillows and quilt blanket. 44⅐ x 44⅞ x 37⅛". Casa Nova
54. Lounge chair. Metal extrusion fixed finish frame; separate seat and back cushions of foam with Dacron wrap over rubber and steel suspension. 32¾ x 33¼ x 28¼". Settee and sofa also available. Knoll International
55. Arm and armless chair. Metal extrusion fixed finish frame; foam cushion bonded to curved laminated plywood shell. Armless chair 21 x 21 x 31¾"; armchair 22½ x 20¾ x 31¾". Knoll International
56. Coffee table. Marble; polished finish base and top. 44¾ x 44¾ x 14½". Knoll International
57. *Serie Locus Solus*. Sunbathing deck chair. Frame of plastified white steel tubing; upholstered parts covered with exclusive printed fabric. 82 x 27¼ x 23". Zanotta

58. *Serie Locus Solus*. Table. Frame of plastified white steel tubing; top in glass. 32¾ x 32¾ x 27¹/₁₀″. Zanotta

59. *Serie Locus Solus*. Armchair. 28½ x 37 x 32″. Zanotta

60. *Serie Locus Solus*. Small sofa. 41⅓ x 20¾ x 25¾″. Zanotta

61. *Serie Locus Solus*. Chair. 21¾ x 21¾ x 25¾″. Zanotta

62. *Serie Locus Solus*. Stool. 21¾ x 21¾ x 19½″. Zanotta

63. *Pipistrella*. Desk lamp. Plastic and metal. Diameter 27½″; height 28⅞″. Martinelli-Luce

64. *Serie April*. Folding chair. Frame of stainless steel; covering of "Tela Strong," Vistram, or leather. 20 ⅓ x 20½ x 31¼″. Zanotta

65. *Serie April*. Folding stool. Frame of stainless steel; covering of "Tela Strong," Vistram, or leather. 22¼ x 17⅛ x 27⅓″. Zanotta

66. *Oracolo*. Table lamp. Metal. Diameter 17½″; height 56⅞″; 40 or 75 watts. Artemide

67. *Minibox*. Swiveling table lamp. Low tension, lacquered metal; reflector fastened by magnet-built-in transformer and 20-watt halogen bulb. Width 6¼″; depth 3⅞″. Stilnovo

68. *Minibox*. Swiveling wall lamp. Low tension, lacquered metal; reflector fastened by magnet-built-in transformer. Width 39″; height 3⅞″. Stilnovo

69/70. *Medusa*. Floor and table lamp. Low tension, chrome-plated metal; reflector fastened by magnet-built-in transformer and 20-watt halogen bulb. Stilnovo

71. *Tea service*. Five pieces and tray. Silver 800. Tray 20¼ x 9¾ x 6¼″. Rossi & Arcandi

72. *Serie Otto A*. Door hardware and coat hooks. Cast brass, gold, chromium, or Nerox. Fusital

73. *Pileno*. Table lamp. White plastic. Width 8⅝″; height 9¾″. Artemide

74. *Rimorchiatore*. Table lamp. White metal; 40- and 100-watt bulb. Width 12¼″; height 14¼″. Candle

75. *Solus*. Chair. Frame of stainless steel; upholstered seat covered with fabric or leather. 21¾ x 21¾ x 25¾″. Zanotta

76. *Gruppo Stringa*. Two- or three-seat sofas. Chrome frame; outside back covered with fabric or leather; cushions in leather. Poltronova

77. *Gruppo Stringa*. Armchair. Chrome frame; outside back covered with fabric or leather; cushions in leather. Poltronova

78. *Gruppo Stringa*. Low tables. Chrome frame with top in walnut or smoked glass. Poltronova

79. *Gaetano*. Trestle. Frame of aluminum alloy anodized natural or white; rubber hand grips. 27½ x 19⅛ x 27⅜″. Zanotta

80. *Gaetano*. Working table. Top of tempered glass with or without red border or white plastic laminate. 58½ x 29¼ x 27¾″. Zanotta

81. *Bettino*. Single bed. Ash frame, natural color; springing surface of plywood strips; head and foot boards of uni-board, parchment color. 46⅞ x 79⅞ x 27¼″. Zanotta

82. *Festo*. Low table. Dismountable frame of aluminum anodized natural or black; top of tempered glass. 31¼ x 31¼ x 28″. Zanotta

83. *Festo*. Console. Dismountable frame of aluminum anodized natural or black; top of tempered glass. 50¾ x 15⅝ x 32″. Zanotta

84. *Tripolina*. Dismountable easy chair. Frame of stainless steel; covering of "Tela Strong." 27⅓ x 27⅓ x 41⅓″. Zanotta

85. *Mezzoracolo*. Table lamp. Glass and metal. Diameter 17½″; height 26½″. Artemide

86. *Patroclo*. Table lamp. Glass and steel. Diameter 18⅜″; height 15⅜″. Artemide

1

2

3

4

5

6

7

8

9

10

11

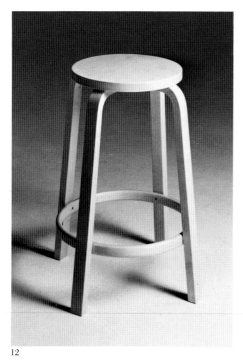

12

13

14

15

16

17

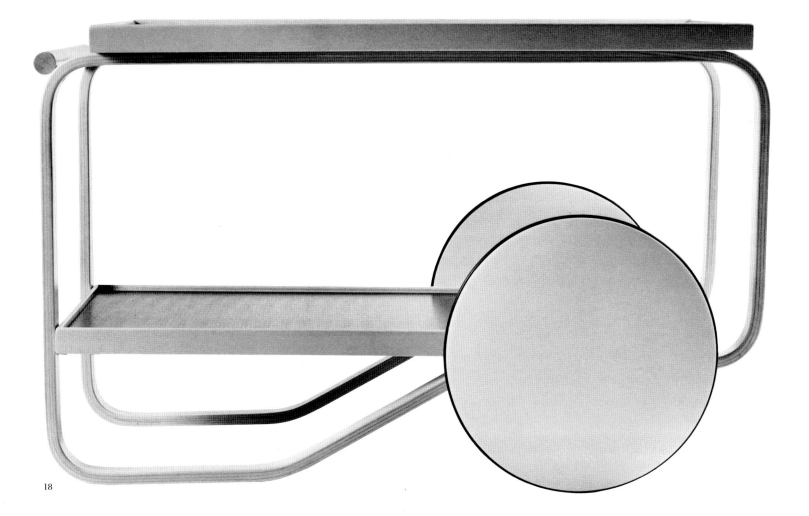

18

19

20

21

22

23

24

25

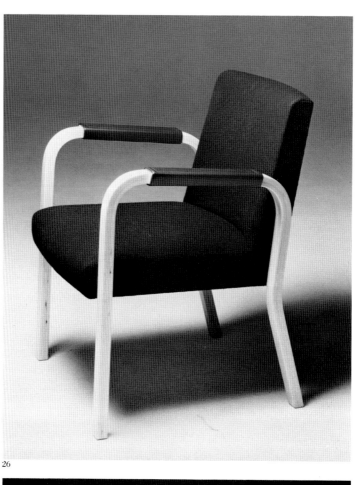

26

27

28

29

30

31

32

33

34

35

36

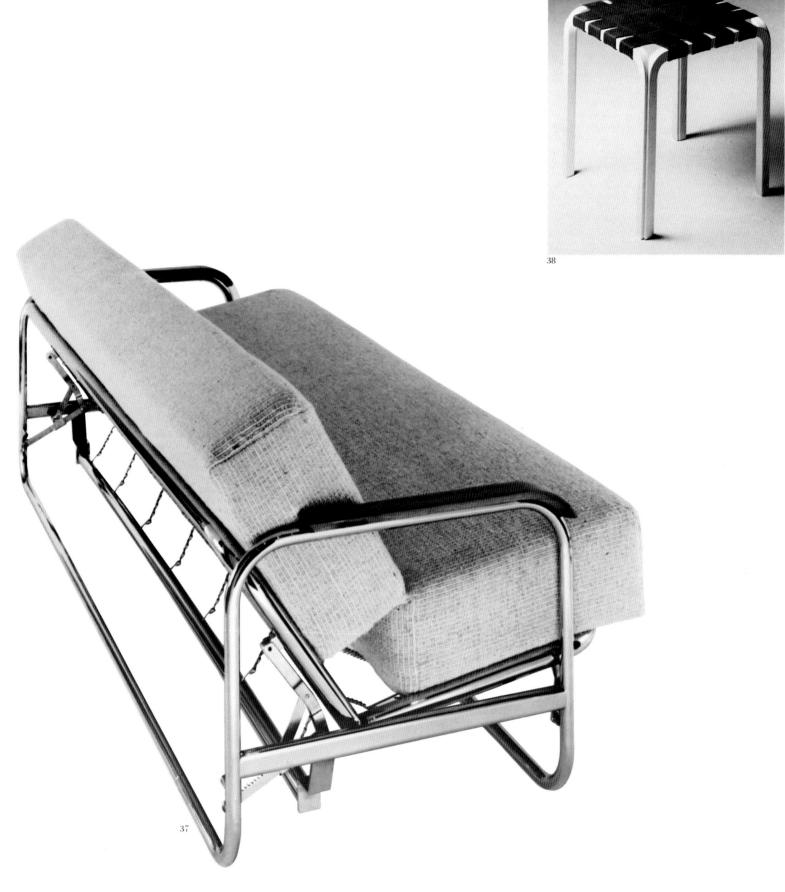

38

37

39

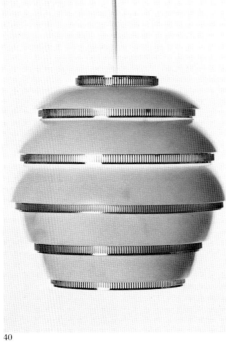

40

41

43

42

44

45

46

47

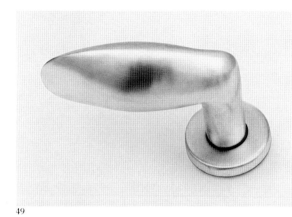

49

50

51

52

52

53

53

54

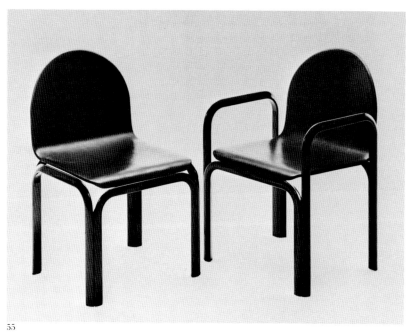

55

56

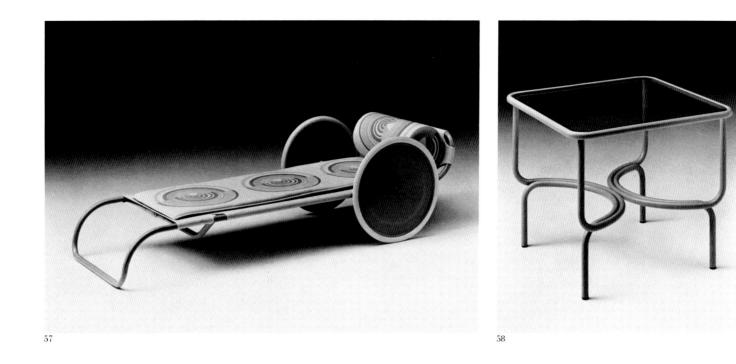

57

58

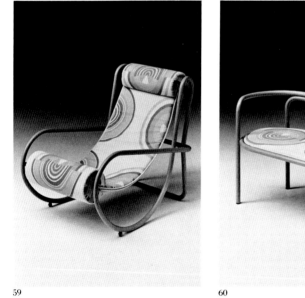

59

60

61

62

63

64

65

66

67

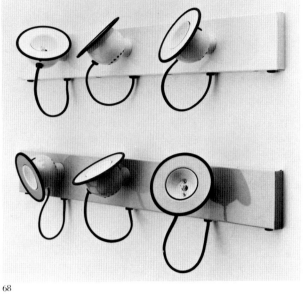

68

69

70

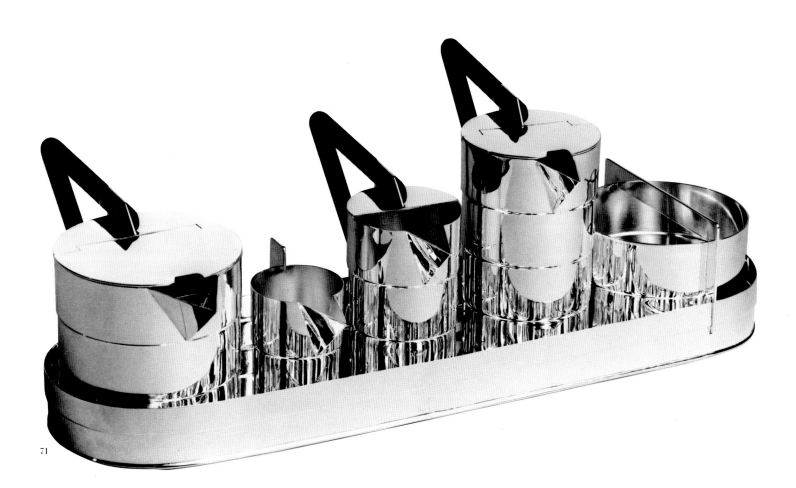

71

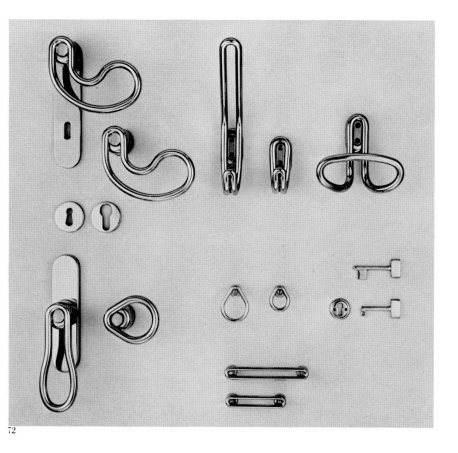

72

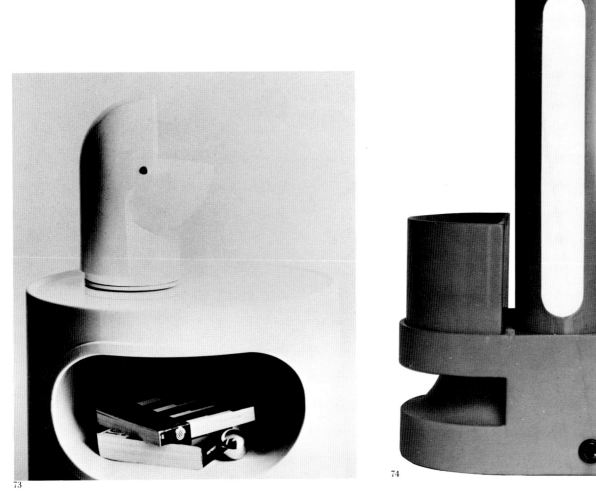

73

74

75

76

77

78

79

81

80

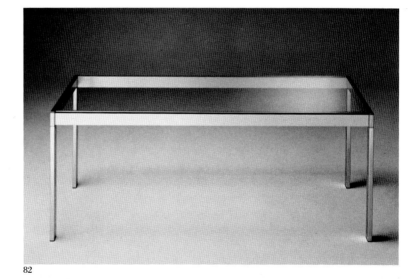

82

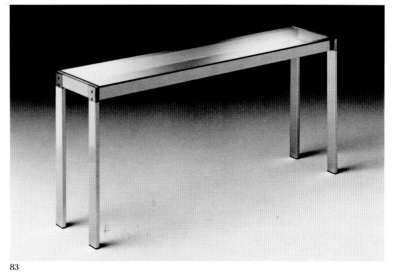

83

84

85

86

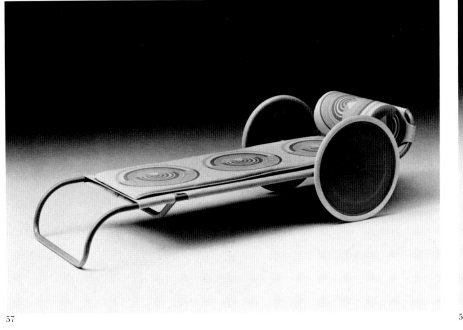

57

58

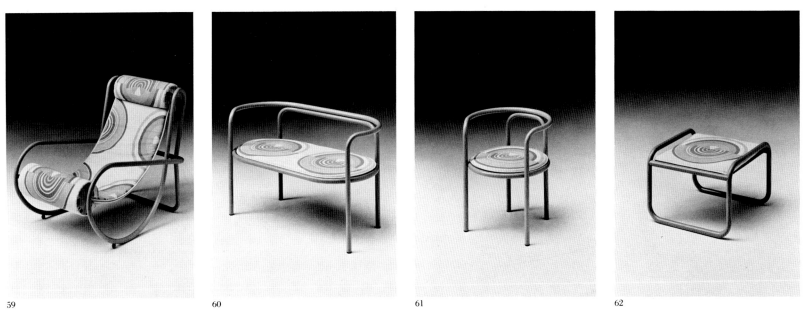

59

60

61

62

63

64

65

66

67

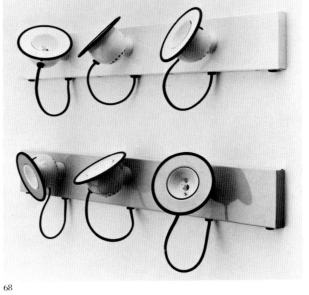

68

69

70

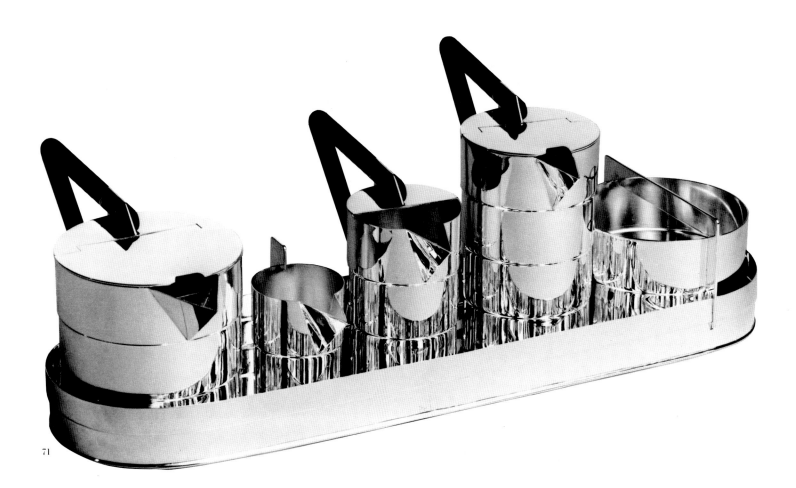

71

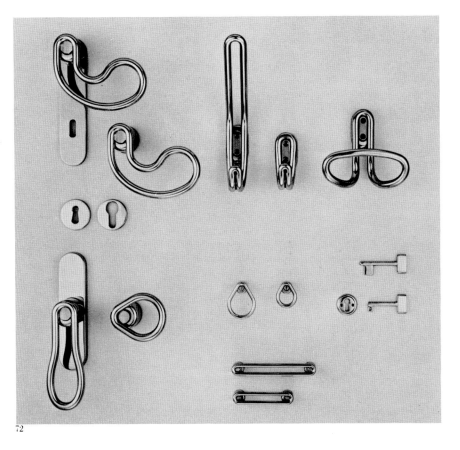

72

73

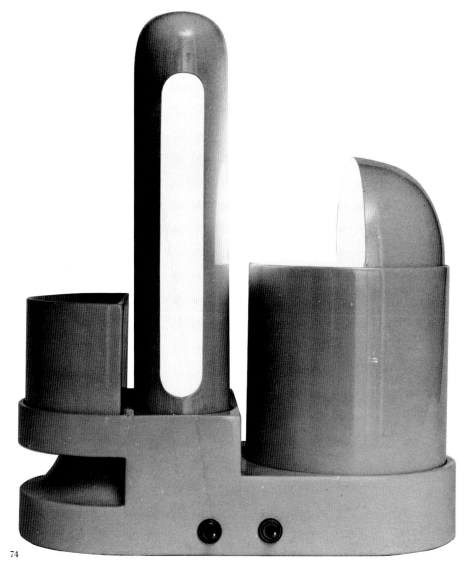

74

75

76

77

78

81

79

80

82

83

84

85

86

B

BBPR

Max Bill

Luigi Blau

Marcel Breuer

André Bruyère

BBPR Gianluigi Banfi (1910–1945); Lodovico Belgiojoso (b. 1909); Enrico Peressutti (1908–1973); and Ernesto Rogers (1909–1969)

Founded in Italy in 1932, the group BBPR considered the field of architecture to include the designing of everything "from teaspoon design to regional planning." Such a comprehensive approach led the group—already famous in prewar Italy—to tackle such diverse projects as the Torre Velasca in Milan, the Olivetti store in New York, and the urban development plan of Canzo, Italy.

87. *Velasca.* Door handle. Brass. Length 4⅝″. Window handle also available. Olivari
88. *Emma.* Door handle. Brass. Length 6″. Window handle also available. Olivari
89. *Melpomēne.* Coat tree. Chromium-plated brass. Base diameter 15⅞″; height 70¼″. Artemide

Max Bill (b. 1908)

Swiss architect, writer, painter, industrial designer, and sculptor, Max Bill's works bear the hallmark of a two-year stay at the Bauhaus in Dessau in the late 1920s. Later he served as director (1953–57) of the Ulm Hochschule für Gestaltung, an institution that influenced postwar German design. Bill's diverse interests in the architectural field include his famous Lavina-Tobel bridge in Switzerland, the wind column of the Montreal Musée d'Art Contemporain, and the prefabricated timber prototype house in Beremgasten, Switzerland.

90. *Scabilo.* Stool. 1950. Stratified birch structure. 15⅝ x 11⅛ x 17½″. Zanotta
91. Stool. 1954. Massive fir, varnished. 17½ x 11¾ x 15⅝″. Holzwerkstätten
92. Dismountable table. Black aluminum castors, hornbeam. 27⅜ x 27⅜ x 25⅞″. Holzwerkstätten

Luigi Blau (b. 1945)

A Viennese architect who apprehends furniture design as part of his everyday architectural practice, Luigi Blau considers the most basic projects—a one-family house, a chair—to be sources of possible innovation. Despite its apparent simplicity, Blau's furniture shows that ordinary objects can always—despite their common material—be improved.

93. Chair. Massive beech, redwood color; transparent varnish. 20½ x 16⅜ x 35½″. Holzwerkstätten
94. *Dutch Table 1.* Table. Massive beech, legs in maple; transparent varnish. 80⅜ x 37½ x 29¼″. Holzwerkstätten
95. *Dutch Table 2.* Table. Legs in massive beech; top covered with linoleum and framed with beech. 56⅛ x 33⅛ x 29¼″. Holzwerkstätten
96. *Dutch Table 3.* Square table. Legs in maple; top covered with linoleum and framed with beech. 33⅛ x 33⅛ x 29¼″. Can be combined with #97. Holzwerkstätten
97. *Dutch Table 4.* Folding table. Legs in maple; top covered with linoleum and framed with beech. 33⅛ x 33⅛ x 29¼″. Can be combined with #96. Holzwerkstätten

Marcel Breuer (1902–1982)

Throughout his professional life the world-famous furniture-maker and architect Marcel Breuer applied to his designs the principles and concepts he learned, and later taught, at the Weimar Bauhaus. There under his direction, the furniture design section shifted from an Arts and Crafts approach to a bolder exploration of the ways mass production could be applied to problems of design. His experiments with modular and tubular furniture were the first of their kind and revolutionized the furniture design industries in Europe and the United States (where he emigrated in 1937). Breuer's architecture included family houses and cottages as well as major commissions such as the UNESCO headquarters in Paris, the Whitney Museum of American Art in New York, and St. John's Abbey Church in Minnesota.

98. *Wassily.* Lounge chair. 1925. Frame in tubular steel, polished chrome finish; upholstery in leather or canvas. 30¾ x 27 x 28½″. Knoll International

99. *Cesca*. Armless chair. 1928. Frame in tubular steel, polished chrome finish; seat in hand-woven or machine-woven cane or upholstered with fabric, vinyl, or leather. 18¼ x 22⅝ x 31¼". Knoll International

100. *Cesca*. Armchair. 1928. Frame in tubular steel, polished chrome finish; seat in hand-woven or machine-woven cane or upholstered with fabric, vinyl, or leather. 22⅝ x 22⅝ x 31¾". Knoll International

101. Lounge chair. 1928. Frame in tubular steel, polished chrome finish; seat covered with wickerwork; armrest made of wood. 25⅝ x 32⅜ x 32¼". Armchair also available. Thonet (West Germany)

102. *Laccio*. Table. 1925–26. Base in tubular steel with polished chrome finish; top in plastic laminate. 53½ x 18⅞ x 13⅜". Knoll International

103. Writing desk. Frame in tubular steel, polished chrome finish; drawers in wood. 63⅞ x 29⅝ x 28½". Thonet (West Germany)

104. Writing desk. Frame in tubular steel, polished chrome finish; drawers in wood. 39¾ x 19½ x 25⅝". Thonet (West Germany)

105. Occasional tables. Frame in tubular steel, polished chrome finish; top in wood. 25⅝ x 17½ x 17½"; 23⅜ x 17½ x 19½". Thonet (West Germany)

106. Folding armchair. 1926. Frame in tubular steel; seat and back in canvas. 27¼ x 30 x 23⅜". Tecta

107. Sofa. 1930–31. Frame in tubular steel and flat steel bars; upholstered cushions. Tecta

108. Cupboard. 1925. Tecta

109. Stonehenge conference table. 1980. Two bases; granite. 48 x 96 x 29". ICF (U.S.)

110. Side chair. Tubular steel frame in mirror-polished chrome plating; five powder-coated finish colors or brass finish; maplewood finger-jointed seat/back frames. 18¼ x 22½ x 32". Thonet (U.S.)

111. Armchair. Tubular steel frame in mirror-polished chrome plating; five powder-coated finish colors or brass finish; maplewood finger-jointed seat/back frames and armrests. 23 x 22½ x 32". Thonet (U.S.)

112. *Wassily*. Chair. 1925. Polished chrome-plated tubular steel frame; natural, deep brown, or black leather seat, back straps, and arm straps. 31 x 28½ x 28½". Thonet (U.S.)

André Bruyère (b. 1912)

Strong surrealistic influences and a sure knack for poetry and poetic spatial experiments led the French architect André Bruyère to radically reject the systematic and geometric architectural credos that prevailed in postwar Europe and America. Such attitudes, however, did not prevent him from designing bank offices, vacation resorts, private homes, and technical facilities.

Bruyère's furniture and objects are, like his architecture, designed with a specialized sense of refined forms and natural materials.

113. Table. Base in stainless steel; top in wood and brass, marble, or glass. André Bruyère Editions

114. Chest. Wood with precious wood veneer. André Bruyère Editions

115. *Aurelien*. Bench. Wood. André Bruyère Editions

116. *A La Portee Du Merveilleux*. Magnifier. Steel and glass. André Bruyère Editions

117. *Spirale D'archimede*. Table lamp. Glass globe and Plexiglas; halogen bulb. André Bruyère Editions

118. *Lampadaire Plein Feu*. Floor lamp. Black steel sheet and steel tubing. André Bruyère Editions

119. *Soleil Sur Tige*. Floor or table lamp. Steel and aluminum. André Bruyère Editions

120. *Boite Magnifique*. Light box. Polished brass or stainless steel; magnifier. André Bruyère Editions

121. *Penetrer La Parabole*. Magnifier. Wood and glass. André Bruyère Editions

122. Washbasin. Marble. André Bruyère Editions

123. Washbasin. Marble with brass faucet. André Bruyère Editions

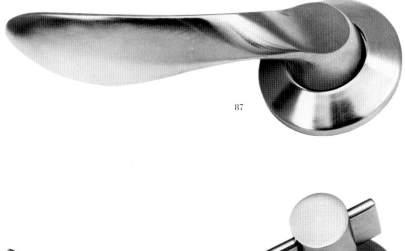

87

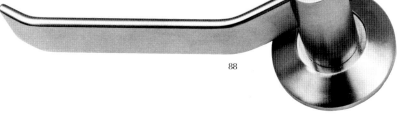

88

89

91

92

90

94

95

96

97

97

96 97

99

98

100

101

102

103

104

106

105

107 108

109

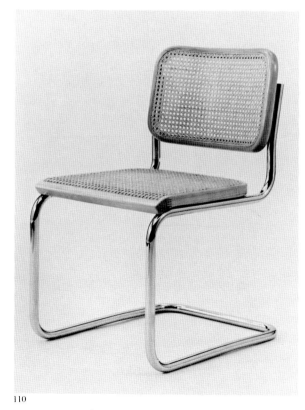

110

111

112

113

114

115

116

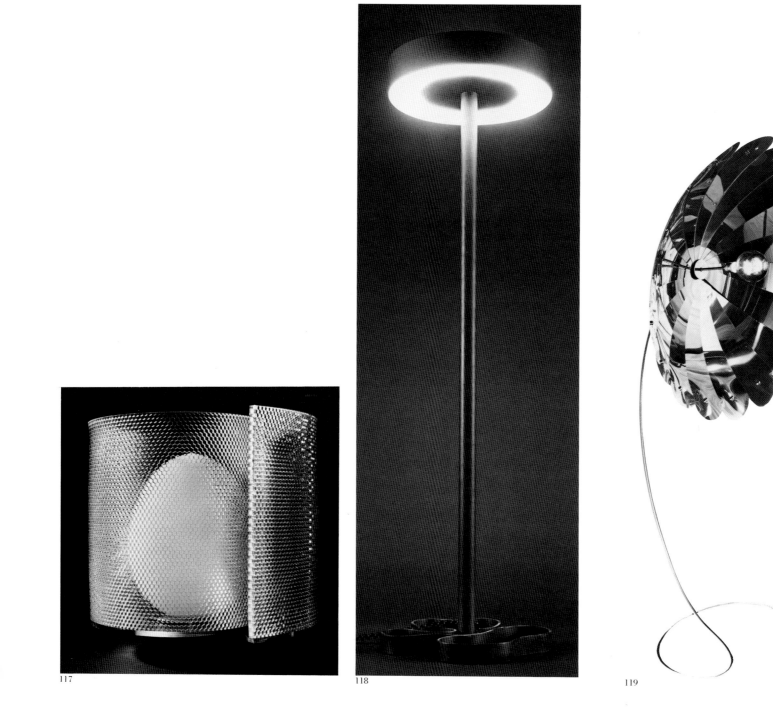

117

118

119

120

121

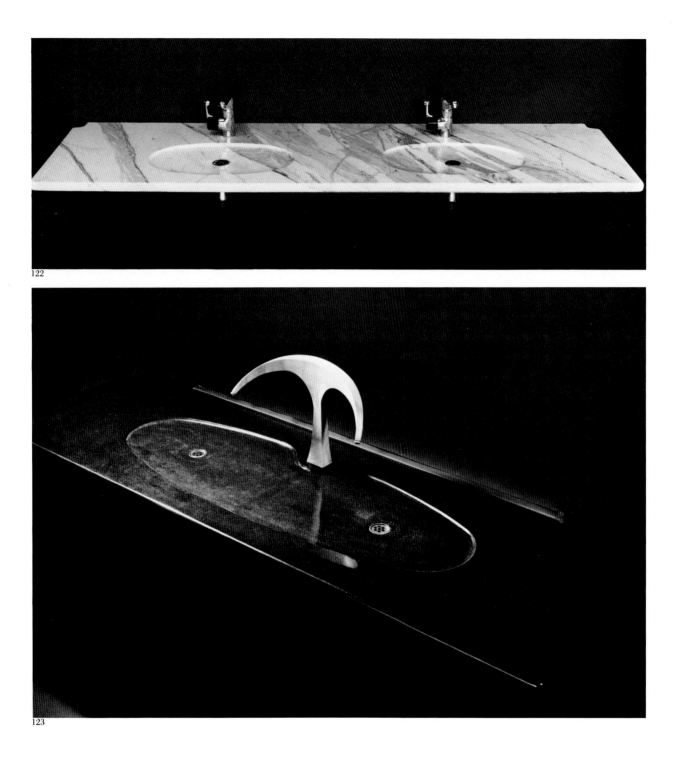

122

123

CDE

Hans Coray

Le Corbusier, Pierre Jeanneret,
and Charlotte Perriand

Hans Dissing and Otto Weitling

Charles Eames

Hans Coray

*Best known for his aluminum chair designed in
1938 for the Swiss National Exhibition, the Swiss
architect Hans Coray employed innovatively the
latest metallurgy processes of the time.*

124. *Spartana.* Stacking chair. 1938. Canadian aluminum alloy frame treated by special process. 21 x
25⅛ x 29½". Zanotta
125. *Landa.* Stacking chair. 1952. Seat and back,
with or without holes, of bent plywood or beech,
natural or white lacquered. 18¾ x 19⅞ x 31¼".
Zanotta

Le Corbusier (Charles-Edouard Jeanneret)
(1887–1965)
Pierre Jeanneret (1896–1967)
Charlotte Perriand (b. 1903)

*The most revered and controversial architect of the
modern period, the genius whose few writings and
buildings drastically influenced the architectural
and urban-design philosophies of our times, Le
Corbusier was, to his very last days, a man of order,
precision, and sensitivity. Born and raised in La
Chaud de Fond, Le Corbusier traveled throughout
Europe before settling in Paris. There he came to
question the obsolete academicism of the European
architectural establishment and prophesized an industrial world with a new order of social, political,
economic, aesthetic, and architectural implications.*

*Le Corbusier considered the field of architecture
unlimited and the role of architect to be that of total
designer. He designed luxury cars for the automo-
bile industry, controversial master plans for Paris,
expensive houses, and industrialized collective low-
cost housing. Among his well-known works are the
Villa Savoye in Poissy, France; Notre-Dame-du-
Haut Chapel in Ronchamp, France; and the Carpenter Center for the Visual Arts at Harvard University.*

*Le Corbusier's interest in furniture design devel-
oped when his first-cousin Pierre Jeanneret and a
young, talented designer, Charlotte Perriand, joined
the atelier to produce a small series of tables,
armchairs, sofas, and cabinets that could be mass-
produced and sold inexpensively. It was not, however,
until the early 1960s that the furniture industry
discovered the furniture's qualities and commercial
potentialities and decided to mass-produce it as Le
Corbusier had masterfully envisioned years before.*

126. *LC 1.* Sling chair. 1928. Frame in highly polished
tubing; seat and back in special fabric, Russian
leather, or hairy skin. 23⅝ x 25⅝ x 25¼".
Cassina
127. *LC 4.* Chaise lounge. 1928–29. Frame in highly
polished chrome-plated tubing with webbed
springs; subframe in lacquered webbed steel;
seat and back with rubber straps with high
tensile strength coiled springs; upholstery in pony
skin or leather. Width 22¼"; depth 63". Cassina
128. *LC 3.* Two-seat sofa. 1928. Frame in highly
polished tubing; seat and back with rubber straps
surrounding steel springs; cushions in a combination of polyurethane, foam, latex, and rubberized
cocoa fibers; cover in fabric, vinyl, or leathers.
61⅛ x 28⅞ x 24⅜". Cassina
129. *LC 2.* Armchair. 1928–29. Frame in highly
polished tubing; seat and back with rubber straps
surrounding steel springs; cushions in a combination of polyurethane, foam, latex, and rubberized
cocoa fibers; cover in fabric, vinyl, or leathers.
27½ x 29⅞ x 26⅜". Cassina
130. *LC 6.* Table. 1925–28. Enameled steel base top
available in crystal or ashwood with a natural or
black-ebonized finish. 90 x 33½ x 27⅛". Cassina
131. *LC 9.* Bath stool. 1925–28. Polished chrome-
plated frame; upholstered with fabric. 19¾ x
14⅛ x 17¾". Cassina
132. *LC 8.* Stool. 1925–28. Polished chrome-plated or
colored enamel steel frame; cushion padded with
polyurethane and upholstered in fabric, vinyl, or
leather. Diameter 18½"; height 19¾". Cassina
133. *LC 7.* Revolving armchair. 1925–28. Polished
chrome-plated or colored enamel steel frame;
back and seat cushions padded with polyurethane and upholstered in fabric, vinyl, or leather.
23⅝ x 19⅞ x 28⅞". Cassina
134. *Casiers Standard.* Modular container units. 1935.
Ash-stained walnut or colored finish with solid
wood edges. Widths 14⅝", 29¼", 43⅞"; depths
14⅝", 29¼". Cassina
135. *Salubra.* Wallpaper. Available in eight colors.
Salubra-Viacroze

Hans Dissing
Otto Weitling

*After the death of the Danish architect Arne Jacobsen
in 1971, his successors, Hans Dissing and Otto
Weitling, continued to run this master's firm and to
finish his ongoing work, the Danish National
Bank. Since that time these two architects have
gone further and designed many public and semipub-*

lic projects, among them the interior of the Copenhagen Central Station. Today this firm is considered
one of the best architectural firms in Denmark.

136. *D W Globe.* Outdoor lamp. U-formed, nonprotected
aluminum pole; globe of opal polycarbonate;
200-watt incandescent or 125-watt mercury bulb.
Height 109¼″. Louis Poulsen

137. *D W Cylinder Lamp.* Outdoor lamp. U-formed
nonprotected aluminum pole; cylinder housing
and wire guard of sand-blast silicium casting;
light source cover of opal polycarbonate; 200-watt
incandescent or 80-watt mercury lamp. Height
40⅞″. Louis Poulsen

Charles Eames (1907–1978)

*In 1940 the American architect and designer Charles
Eames, along with Eero Saarinen, won the "Organic
Design in Home Furnishing" competition spon-
sored by The Museum of Modern Art in New York.
For the next thirty years, Eames designed chairs—in
addition to his well-known house in California
—that became American classics. Experimenting
with plywood, fiberglass, and light metal, Eames
used his wit and his talents to question the rigid
notions of contemporary modern design and to
interject through his furniture the concepts of fantasy
and fun into everyday life.*

138. *Eames® Chaise.* Chaise lounge. 1960. Colored
nylon-coated frame and base; nylon glides; thick
cushions of urethane foam enclosed by polyester
fiber batting and upholstered in top grain leather
in black. 17½ x 75 x 28¾″. Herman Miller

139. *Eames® Sofa Compact.* Sofa. 1954. Bright
chrome-plated legs with black enameled frame;
stainless steel glides; upholstered spring-supported
urethane foam cushions. 72½ x 29⅞ x 34⅞″.
Herman Miller and ICF (Italy)

140. *Eames® Lounge Chair and Ottoman.* Lounge chair
and ottoman. 1956. Seat, back, and ottoman
shells in molded Brazilian rosewood veneer;
black enameled bases and back braces with
bright-polished aluminum trim; upholstered in
top grain leather in colors. Lounge 32½ x 32¾ x
33⅜″; ottoman 26 x 21 x 15″. Herman Miller

141. *Eames® Four-Legged Base Chair.* Dining-room
chair. 1946. Plywood walnut veneer or fiberglass-
reinforced plastic shell seat and back with or
without upholstery; bright chrome-plated base
and back support. 18½ x 22 x 31¼″. Herman
Miller

142. *Eames® Executive Seating.* Lounge chair. 1960.
Bright-polished aluminum base and frame; back
seat and armrest upholstered and padded; tilt
swivel; available with glides or castors. With
glides as shown 26½ x 27 x 32½″. Herman
Miller

143. *Eames® Stacking and Ganging Chair.* Chair.
Fiberglass-reinforced plastic side shell; bright
tubular steel legs; side braces, hooks, and loops
of bright-plated steel rods; self-leveling white
nylon glides; upholstered or nonupholstered.
23½ x 21½ x 31¾″. Herman Miller

144. *Eames® Tandem Shell Seating.* Chair. Fiberglass-
reinforced plastic armshell; four-leg or wallguard
base; upholstered or nonupholstered. 24⅞ x 24 x
31″. Herman Miller

145. *Eames® Shell Chair.* Chair. 1971. Fiberglass-
reinforced plastic side shell; bright-polished aluminum base; swivel or nonswivel; upholstered or
nonupholstered. 18½ x 22 x 32¼″. Herman
Miller

146. *Eames® Aluminum Group.* Side pull-up chair.
Upholstered; with or without arms; bright-
polished aluminum base, armrests, and frame;
dark tone column. 22 x 28½ x 33¾″. Herman
Miller

147. *Eames® Tandem Sling Seating.* Seat units. 1962.
Polished aluminum base; black steel bars; padded
vinyl. Herman Miller

148. *Eames® Soft Pad Group.* Executive armchair.
1969. Upholstered cushions of urethane foam
enclosed by polyester fiber batting; bright-
polished aluminum base, armrests, and frame;
dark tone column with tilt-swivel mechanism;
castors. 22½ x 23¾ x 40″. Herman Miller

149. *Eames® Soft Pad Group.* Side pull-up chair. Upholstered cushions of urethane foam enclosed by
polyester fiber batting; with or without arms;
bright-polished aluminum base, armrests, and
frame; dark tone column. 21 x 24 x 34″. Herman
Miller

150. *Eames® Soft Pad Group.* Reclining chair. Upholstered cushions of urethane foam enclosed by
polyester fiber batting; with or without arms;
bright-polished aluminum base, armrests, and
frame; dark tone column. 22 x 29¼ x 34½″.
Herman Miller

151. *Segmented Base Table.* Table. Bright-polished
aluminum legs; dark tone columns, stretchers,
and vinyl edge; top in hardwood veneer or plastic
laminate faced. 60 x 30 x 28½″. Herman Miller

124

125

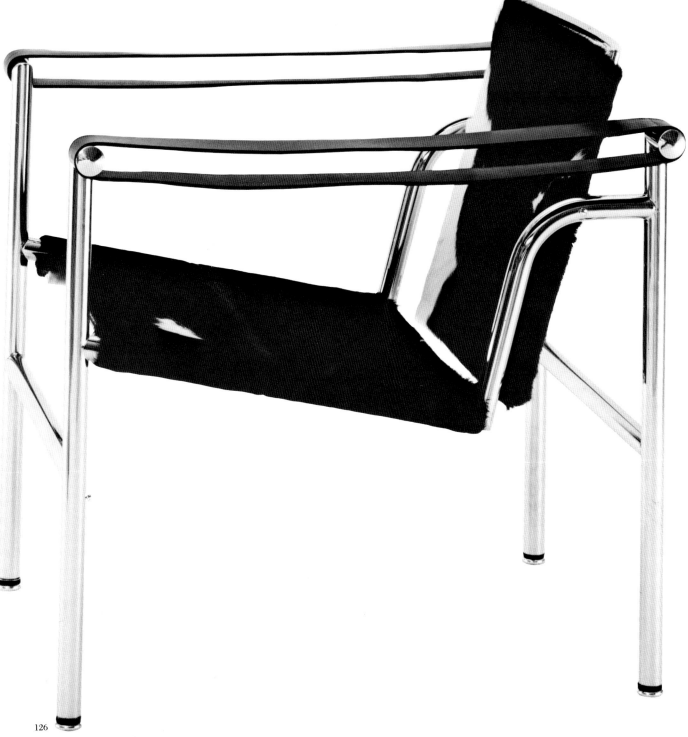

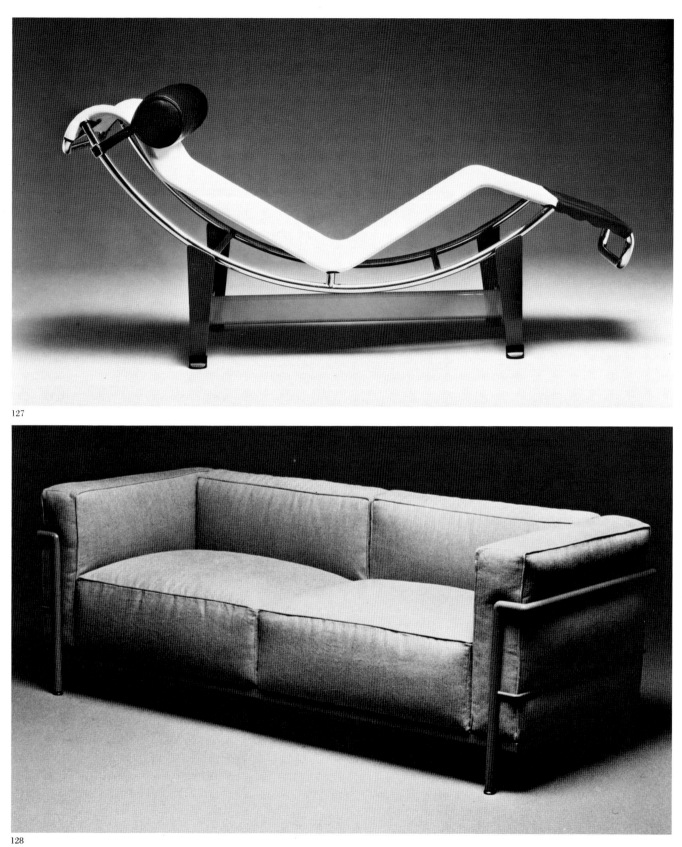

127

128

131

130

136 137

138

139

140

141

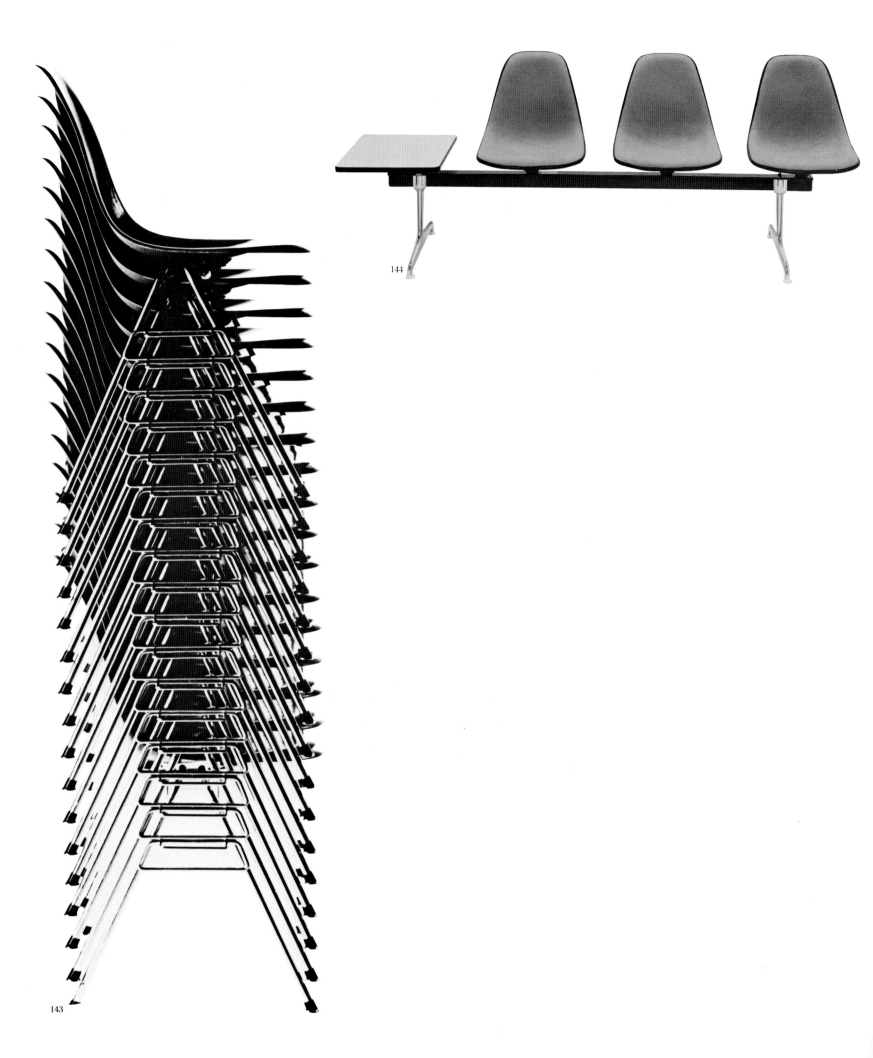

143

144

146

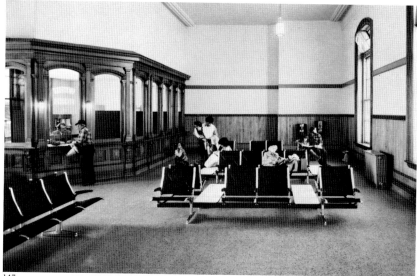

147

145

148

149

150

151

G

Piero Gatti, Cesare Paolini,

and Franco Teodoro

Antonio Gaudí

Frank O. Gehry

Michael Graves

Eileen Gray

Vittorio Gregotti

Walter Gropius

GRUPPO ARCHITETTI URBANISTI CITTA NUOVA

Hans Gugelot

Charles Gwathmey and Robert Siegel

**Piero Gatti
Cesare Paolini
Franco Teodoro**

A trio of young Italian architects whose Sacco seat bag was a simple but efficient concept that rapidly turned into a best-selling item.

152. *Sudanese.* Folding cot. Structure of kiln-dried beech, natural color; joints of lacquered steel; removable covering of "Tela Strong." 29¼ x 75⅝ x 15⅞". Zanotta

153. *Sacco.* Easy chair. 1969. Envelope of Nailpelle, fabric, or leather, containing highly resistant polystyrene pellets. 31¼ x 31¼ x 26½". Zanotta

Antonio Gaudí (1852–1926)

During his lifetime Antonio Gaudí was little known outside his native Catalonia. However, in the mid-1950s, he was recognized internationally for the nonconventional "free form" structures he built in Barcelona. Behind his exuberant, fantastic concepts resided an authentic architectural wit and technically imaginative genius who was soon acclaimed for his approach as a total architect. Confronted in his early practice with late nineteenth-century romanticism, Gaudí integrated the style of the period with the influence of Art Nouveau and designed buildings that seemed free of form yet were the result of rigorous building rules. One of his most famous is the Church of the Sagrada Familia in Barcelona, which remains unfinished.

Gaudí's furniture and objects demonstrated his concept of architect as total designer. These pieces were originally designed for Barcelona mansions, but in recent times they have been reissued through the careful handwork of Spanish craftsmen.

154. *Calvet Armchair.* Armchair. 1904. American oak, carved with hand-gouge; acid dyeing and varnish with polyurethane wax. B. D. Ediciones

155. *Calvet Stool.* Stool. 1904. American oak, carved with hand-gouge; acid dyeing and varnish with polyurethane wax. B. D. Ediciones

156. *Batlló Chair.* Chair. 1905–7. American oak, carved with hand-gouge; acid dyeing and varnish with polyurethane wax. B. D. Ediciones

157. *Batlló Bench.* Bench. 1905–7. American oak, carved with hand-gouge; acid dyeing and varnish with polyurethane wax. B. D. Ediciones

158. *Calvet Mirror.* Mirror. 1904. American oak, carved with hand-gouge; acid dyeing and varnish with polyurethane wax. B. D. Ediciones

159. *Pull Mila.* Pull. 1910. Solid brass, hand polished, protected by transparent glaze. Width 4"; depth 2⅜". B. D. Ediciones

160. *Mila.* Hardware. 1910. Solid brass, hand polished, protected by transparent glaze. B. D. Ediciones

161. *Batlló Pulls.* 1905–7. Solid brass, hand polished, protected by transparent glaze. B. D. Ediciones

162. TOP: *Batlló Door Handle.* 1905–7. Solid brass, hand polished, protected by transparent glaze. Width 4"; depth 2¼". B. D. Ediciones
BOTTOM: *Mila Door Knob.* 1910. Solid brass, hand polished, protected by transparent glaze. Width 1⅞"; depth 1⅞". B. D. Ediciones

163. *Calvet.* Multiple hardware accessories. 1904. Solid brass, hand polished, protected by transparent glaze. B. D. Ediciones

Frank O. Gehry (b. 1929)

Since the early 1970s, the Canadian-born, California-based architect Frank Gehry has challenged American architectural conformism through his masterful collage techniques. "The imagery is real and not abstract," Gehry has written, using distortion and juxtaposition of cheap materials to create surrealistic compositions. Gehry's use of fiberboard in the construction of his furniture expresses, beyond its provocative dimension, a reconsideration of furniture's aesthetics and permanence.

164. *Easy Edges Furniture.* Dining chair. 1971–72. Pressed cardboard. 21 x 15 x 32". Cheru Enterprises

165. *Easy Edges Furniture.* Wiggle dining chair. 1971–72. Pressed cardboard. 23 x 15 x 34". Cheru Enterprises

166. *Easy Edges Furniture.* Rocker. Pressed cardboard. 24 x 40 x 26". Cheru Enterprises

167. *Easy Edges Furniture.* Curved sofa chair. Pressed cardboard. 23½ x 32½ x 29". Cheru Enterprises

Michael Graves (b. 1934)

One of the most influential American architects working today is Michael Graves. His buildings and interiors have been recognized for their rich reliance on classical motifs and color and for the poetic and

metaphorical landscapes they create. One of his most recent and important projects has been the Portland Building in Portland, Oregon.

Graves's additional gifts as a painter have furthermore allowed him to interpret and reinterpret classical and modern European master artists through large murals and small, refined drawings, which have brought him logically to the fields of furniture and fabric design.

168. Lounge chair. 1982. Bird's-eye maple veneer frame with upholstered seat and back. 32 x 29 x 29". Sunar

169. Sofa. 1982. Bird's-eye maple veneer frame with upholstered seat and back. 54 x 30½ x 32". Sunar

170. Table. 1982. Lacquered or wood with veneer pattern; square fragments of bird's-eye maple separated by line of ebony with mother-of-pearl tesserae at corner intersections. 40½ x 40½ x 29". Sunar

171. *Scroll*. Fabric. 1982. Cotton, eight screens, printed or predyed fabric with overprint and discharge printing of the field pattern; flatbed table and discharge printing by hand. Width 54". Sunar

172. *Tracery*. Fabric. 1982. Cotton, six screens, copper rotary print. Width 54". Sunar

173. *Fret*. Fabric. 1982. Cotton, five screens with overprint and discharge printing of the field patterns; flatbed table and discharge printing by hand. Width 54". Sunar

Eileen Gray (1879–1976)

One of the best practitioners of the modern movement, the British architect Eileen Gray developed a personal design touch that involved Art Deco, functional and machine aesthetics, intelligent use of new materials (cork, aluminum, suede, leather), and a fusion of formal and craftsman-oriented skills. Her houses, interiors, and furniture were functional, cleverly conceived, and judiciously elegant, qualities not always present in the bitter architectural manifestos of the 1920s and 1930s.

174. *Transat armchair*. Armchair. Lacquered wood, nickel-plated metal, and leather. 22 x 43 x 31". Ecart International/Pallucco

175. *Satellite*. Mirror. Luminous porthole; enlarging mirror; nickel-plated, metal frame. Diameter 29". Ecart International/Pallucco

176. *Feston*. Rug. 10'5" x 6'7". Ecart International

177. *Black Magic*. Rug. 99 x 89". Ecart International

178. *Mediterranee*. Rug. 11'6" x 5'9". Ecart International

179. *Blackboard* or *Centimetre*. Rug. 1927. 39 x 91". Ecart International

180. *Collage*. Rug. 79 x 63". Ecart International

181. *Tour de Nesle*. Rug. 87 x 75". Ecart International

182. *La Ronde*. Rug. Diameter 87". Ecart International

183. Cabinet. Pivot drawers, lacquered wood, and nickel-plated metal. Ecart International

184. *Jean*. Extensible table. 1927. Polished chromium tubular steel base; white-colored formica top. Drawers closed 24⅞ x 24⅞ x 28⅛"; drawers open 49¾ x 24⅞ x 28⅛". Images (Italy)

185. Wardrobe cabinet. Lacquered wood, nickel-plated metal, and Plexiglas. Ecart International

186. *Lota*. Sofa. 1924. Fully upholstered base and back support on turned feet with four feather-filled loose cushions and seat mattress, all covered in aniline fabric or leather; two box units on castors detachable from sofa ends finished in gloss polyurethane lacquer, front and back black, top and side in contrasting colors. 93⅜ x 34⅜ x 14⅞". Images (Italy)

187. Side table. 1927. Polished chromium-tubular steel frame adjustable to various heights; smoked-glass top. Diameter 19⅞"; adjustable height 23¾–38⅝". Images (Italy)

188. *Bibendum*. Armchair. Polished chromium-plated tubular steel base; fully upholstered seat, back, and armrests covered in aniline fabric or leather. 35⅞ x 31⅞ x 28⅛". Images (Italy)

189. *Roquebrune Chair*. Chair. Tubular chromium steel base; seat and back covered in fabric or in gray, black, white, or natural leather. 17½ x 21½ x 29¼". Images (Italy)

190. *Bonaparte Armchair*. Armchair. Tubular chromium steel base; seat and back upholstered. Images of America

191. Occasional tables. Images of America

192. *Roquebrune Daybed*. Daybed. Tubular chromium steel base; upholstered cushions. Images of America

193. *Tube Light*. Lamp. Polished chromium steel circular base. Height 31¼". Images (Italy)

Vittorio Gregotti (b. 1927)

Italian architect, writer, and magazine editor, Vittorio Gregotti has used his diverse talents and applied them to numerous fields of interest: regional and urban planning, domestic and commercial architecture, furniture and industrial design, and, most recently, to regional universities in Calabria and in Sicily.

194. *Serie Otto G*. Door hardware and coat hooks. Cast brass, gold, chromium, or Nerox. Fusital
195. *Bino* (V. Gregotti, L. Meneghetti, and G. Stoppino). Table lamp. Chrome metal and white metacrylate. Height 21½″; 100-watt bulb. Candle
196. Coffee set. Silver 800. 6⅞ x 14 x 5⅞″. Rossi & Arcandi
197. Shelves and cabinet. Fiberboard covered with varnish or lacquer. 29¼ x 58½ x 91⅝″. B. D. Ediciones
198. *Pesco*. Sofa. Linear frame upholstered with soft wrapping quilt. 33⅛ x 32¾ x 31¼″. Casa Nova
199. *Girasole*. Sofa. Metal frame; quilted upholstery, removable and washable. 67⅛ x 31⅞ x 31¼″. Casa Nova

Walter Gropius (1883–1969)

One of the most famous and innovating architects of the twentieth century as well as its most outstanding architectural teacher, Walter Gropius believed passionately in the unity of design, craft, art, and technology. In 1918, some seven years after his Fagus factory in Alfeld-an-der-Leine had caused a sensation, the German-born Gropius became head of the Bauhaus in Weimar and then in Dessau. At the Bauhaus, Gropius succeeded in erasing the distinction made between the fine and applied arts. His functional approach to design was inextricably bound to its aesthetic contents. After leaving Germany, Gropius became chairman of the architecture department at Harvard and among the projects he designed was the Harvard Graduate Center. It has been written that although the foundation of the modern style had been laid before Gropius, with Gropius "its character was ultimately determined."

200. *The Gropius Service*. Tea service. China, white, black, or colored by Herbert Bayer. Rosenthal
201. Armchair and sofa. Wood and upholstery. Tecta

GRUPPO ARCHITETTI URBANISTI CITTA NUOVA

A group of Italian architects who banded together in the 1950s and then later vanished, their credo affirmed a more humanely built environment in which industrial objects could exist in new, emerging forms of architecture.

202. *Nesso*. Table lamp. White plastic; four 25-watt bulbs. Short lamp diameter 12½″, height 8⅝″; tall lamp diameter 21⅛″, height 13¼″. Artemide

Hans Gugelot (1920–1964)

The originator of new concepts in modular building, the parts of which could be easily mass-produced, the German architect Hans Gugelot experimented with several prefabricated housing systems in Zurich. As part of the German firm Braun, Gugelot set new design standards for house appliances that became the field's reference point for over twenty years.

203. *M-125*. System furniture cabinet. Cupboard with folding doors; frame in natural gaboon, teak, oak, or American walnut; plastic covering. Available in varying widths, depths, and heights. Habit
204. Folding cupboard and partition wall system. Melamined wood covered with light gray paint; top and bottom in steel. Available in varying widths, depths, and heights. D S W

Charles Gwathmey (b. 1938)
Robert Siegel (b. 1939)

One of the best-known architects of his generation, Charles Gwathmey has long been trying to develop, through characteristic buildings, a genuine contemporary American architecture that combines International Style philosophies with the pragmatic and formal achievements of New England vernacular architecture. His handling of volumes and space, remarkable for their poetic geometries, are reflected in the many buildings and residences he has designed with his partner, Robert Siegel. Among the latter are his Haupt Residence in Amagansett, New York; the Benenson Residence in Rye, New York; and the Crowley Residence in Greenwich, Connecticut.

205. Desk with open or closed machine extension. Two-inch top available in different finishes, mahogany an option. Dimensions vary according to style. Knoll International
206a–b. One- or two-pedestal desk. Two-inch top available in different finishes, mahogany an option. Dimensions vary according to style. Knoll International
207. Four-pedestal cabinet. Dimensions vary according to style. Knoll International

153

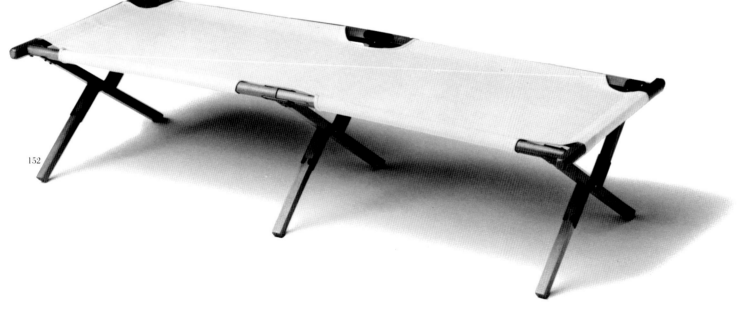

152

154

155

156

157

158

159

160

161

162

163

164

165

166

167

168

169

170

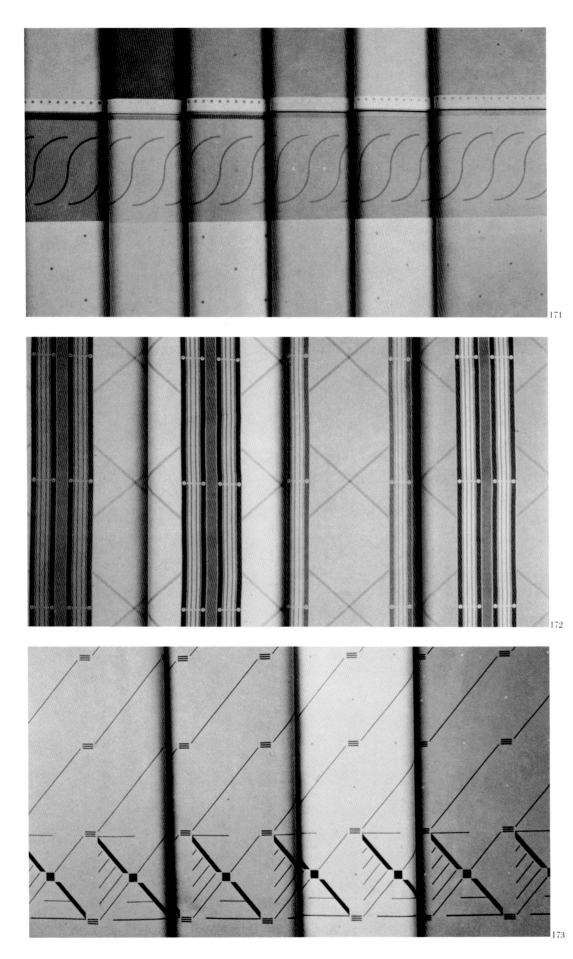

171

172

173

175

174

176

177

178

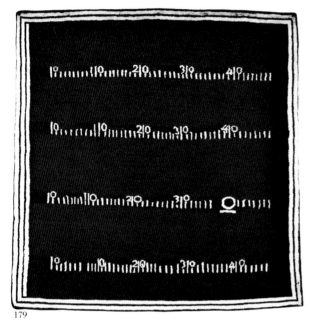

179

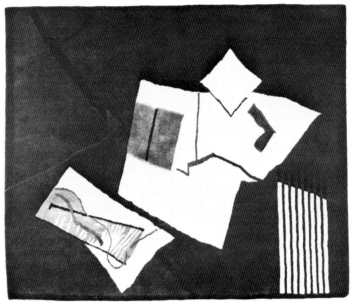

180

181

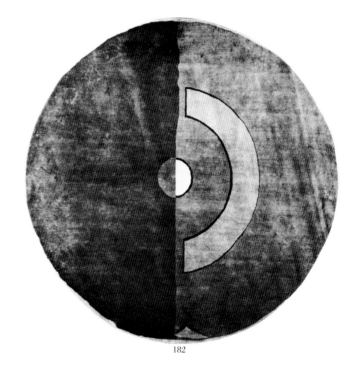

182

183

184

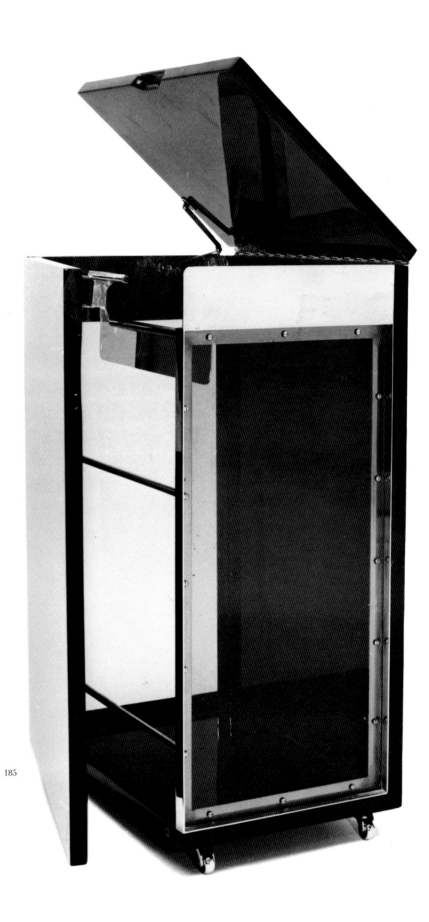

185

186

189

187   188

190

191

192

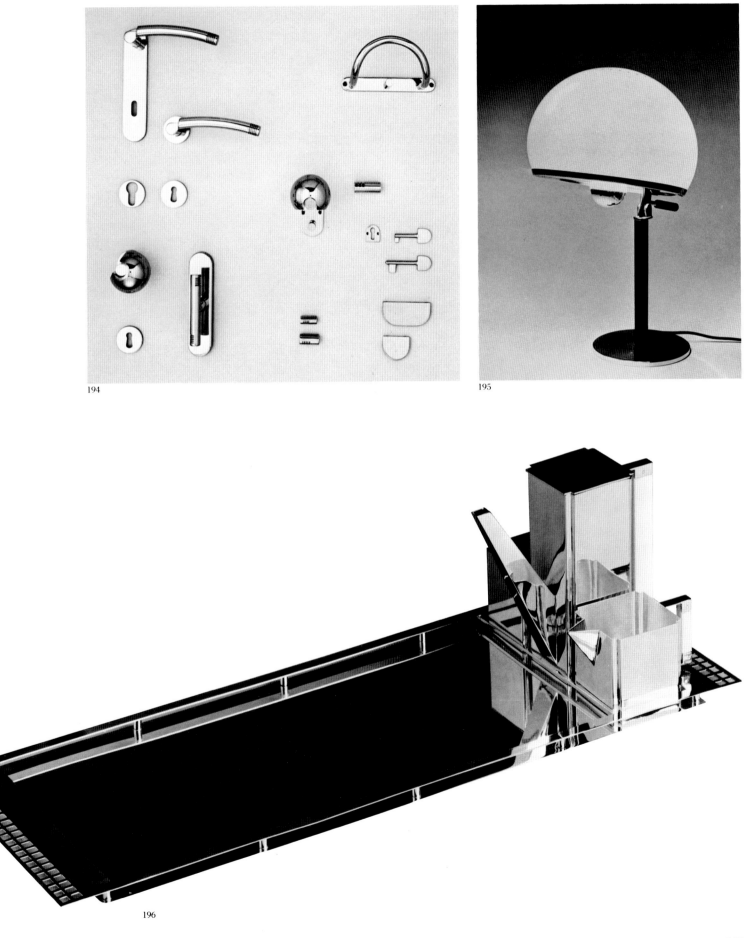

194

195

196

197

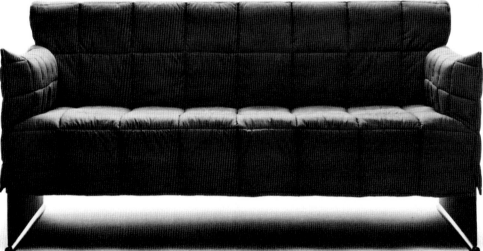

198

199

200

201

202

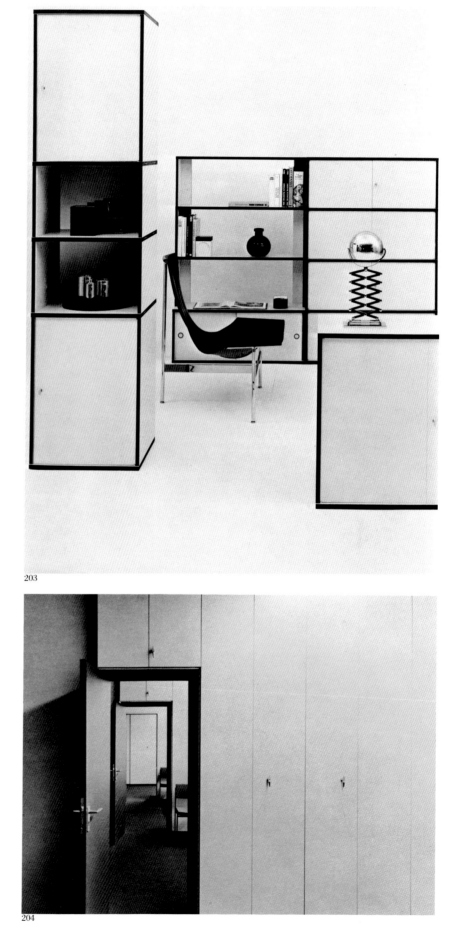

203

204

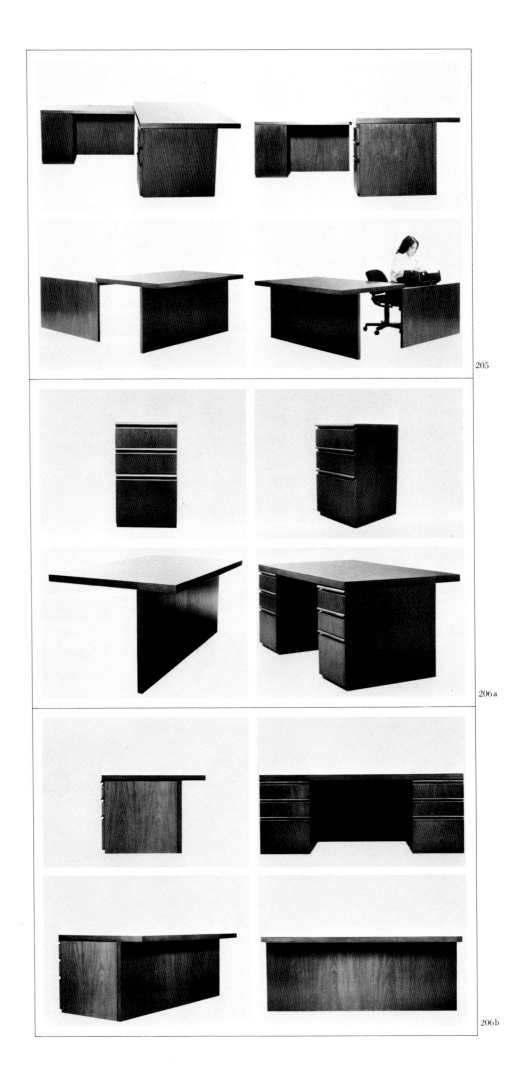

205

206 a

206 b

207

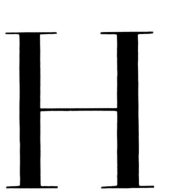

Oswald Haerdtl

Fritz Haller

Ferrari Hardoy, Juan Kurchan,

  and Antonio Bonet

Trix and Robert Haussmann

  and Alfred Hablutzel

René Herbst

Josef Hoffmann

Hans Hollein

Oswald Haerdtl (1889–1959)

In a career that began by his wanting to be a painter, the Austrian architect Oswald Haerdtl soon discovered his gifts as an architect. For several years he worked as Josef Hoffmann's assistant and later became his partner. Together they designed furniture, shops, and public buildings. In 1939 Haerdtl left Hoffmann's office and went out on his own, designing houses and participating in the postwar rebuilding of Vienna.

208.　*Ambassador.* Glass table service. 1925. J & L Lobmeyr

209.　*Carmela.* Glass table service. Salzburger Cristallglass

210.　Candy pot. Glass. J & L Lobmeyr

Fritz Haller (b. 1924)

A practitioner of the modular system approach to architecture, the Swiss architect Fritz Haller has designed numerous office buildings, schools, factories, and collective housing. His philosophy of standardizing industrial elements to be used within a flexible architectural environment has won him recognition throughout the world.

211.　Office furniture system. Frame in chrome tubes and lacquered sheet steel; table top available in wood with different finishes or in marble. Width 15⅜ or 29¼"; depth 19½"; heights 3⅞–29¼". USM

Ferrari Hardoy
Juan Kurchan
Antonio Bonet

In the late 1930s three young Argentinian architects—Antonio Bonet, Juan Kurchan, and Ferrari Hardoy—interested in European modern architecture and Le Corbusier's work, designed an armchair whose simplicity and logic were so evident that almost overnight it became a bestseller. Whether the fact was known to them or not, their innovative idea, minus certain technical refinements, had been patented in 1877 by an American inventor Joseph Fenby, who sold his rights to European manufacturers. The Hardoy chair is so easily produced that today it has been copied numerous times under different names.

212.　*The Hardoy Chair.* Armchair. 1938. Steel and canvas. 28 x 27¼ x 35½". Airborne

Trix Haussmann
Robert Haussmann
Alfred Hablutzel

Masters of texture, pattern design, and trompe l'oeil, *the Zurich architects Trix and Robert Haussmann and their partner, Alfred Hablutzel, have interjected these elements into their architecture. It was not until Post-Modernism, however, that they were able to successfully apply their design techniques, since the puritan ethic of modern architecture rejected the notion of ornament outright. Their interests have led them to the investigation of fabric design and to the designing of shops and handmade furniture in which references to classical architecture are casually expressed with contemporary materials.*

213.　*Mira-Mollitia I Alea.* Fabric. Half-chenille, five colors. Width 50¾". Mira-X

214.　*Mira-Sutura Vimina II.* Fabric. Matelassé, three colors. Width 50¾". Mira-X

215.　*Mira-Sutura Vimina I.* Fabric. Matelassé, three colors. Width 50¾". Mira-X

216.　*Mira-Mollitia II Spina.* Fabric. Velvet chenille, twelve colors. Width 50¾". Mira-X

217.　*Mira-Sutura Spina.* Fabric. Matelassé, three colors. Width 50¾". Mira-X

218.　*Mira-Textura Alea.* Fabric. Damast, one color. Width 50¾". Mira-X

219.　*Mira-Lapideus Squama.* Fabric. Cretonne, four colors. Width 50¾". Mira-X

220.　*Mira-Lapideus Murus.* Fabric. Cretonne, four colors. Width 50¾". Mira-X

221.　*Mira-Marmoreus Columna.* Fabric. Cretonne, six colors. Width 50¾". Mira-X

222.　*Mira-Marmoreus Clatri.* Fabric. Cretonne, six colors. Width 50¾". Mira-X

223.　*Mira-Lapideus Arcola.* Fabric. Cretonne, four colors. Width 50¾". Mira-X

224.　*Mira-Marmoreus Canna.* Fabric. Cretonne, six colors. Width 50¾". Mira-X

225.　*Mira-Ligneus Tabula.* Fabric. Chintz, five colors. Width 53". Mira-X

226.　*Mira-Ligneus Imago.* Fabric. Chintz, four colors; velvet, four colors; Honan silk, five colors. Width 35⅛". Mira-X

227.　*Mira-Ligneus Columna.* Fabric. Honan silk (chintz), five colors. Width 35⅛". Mira-X

228.　*Mira-Ligneus Talus.* Fabric. Batiste, six colors; wool natté, six colors. Width 53". Mira-X

229.　*Mira-Ligneus Vimina.* Fabric. Chintz, five colors; velvet, five colors. Width 53". Mira-X

230. *Mira-Textura Via.* Fabric. Damast, two colors. Width 50¾″. Mira-X

231. *Mira-Textura Murus.* Fabric. Damast, three colors. Width 50¾″. Mira-X

232. *Mira-Pictura I Arcula.* Fabric. Half-linen, one color; voile burn-out, two colors. Width 48¾″. Mira-X

233. *Mira-Pictura II Arcula.* Fabric. Cretonne, one color; voile burn-out, two colors. Width 62⅜″. Mira-X

234. *Mira-Pictura II Canna.* Fabric. Cretonne, one color; voile burn-out, two colors. Width 62⅜″. Mira-X

235. *Mira-Pictura II Adamasi.* Fabric. Cretonne, one color. Width 53⅞″. Mira-X

236. *Mira-Pictura I Adamasi.* Fabric. Half-linen, one color; voile burn-out, two colors. Width 48¾″. Mira-X

237. *Mira-Pictura I Squama.* Fabric. Half-linen, one color; voile burn-out, two colors. Width 48¾″.

238. *Mira-Tomentum Squama.* Fabric. Piqué, six colors. Width 50¾″. Mira-X

239. *Mira-Pellitus Clatri.* Fabric. Velvet, three colors. Width 54⅝″. Mira-X

240. *Mira-Textura Squama.* Fabric. Damast, one color. Width 50¾″. Mira-X

241. *Mira-Junctura Solum.* Fabric. Satin, five colors. Width 49⅞″. Mira-X

242. *Mira-Junctura Alea.* Fabric. Satin, seven colors; batiste, seven colors. Width 49⅞″. Mira-X

René Herbst (1891–1982)

One of the few French modern designers who fought in the 1920s for contemporary furniture design, René Herbst used innovative materials such as aluminum, steel, rubberbands, and Plexiglas for his furniture. Although Herbst's designs and architectural achievements are not numerous, he strongly influenced young designers of the postwar period.

243. Chair. Nickel-plated metal frame; black, white, blue, red, or yellow tension straps. 16⅜ x 15⅝ x 31¼″. Ecart International/Pallucco

244. Chaise lounge. Black-painted or nickel-plated metal frame; black or white tension straps. Ecart International/Pallucco

Josef Hoffmann (1870–1956)

A strong advocate of the integration of the arts, Josef Hoffmann—Austrian architect, craftsman, and designer—helped found, in 1897, the controversial Vienna Secession. Eight years later he left the movement to form the Kunstchau, the "Secession from the Secession."

As a professor of the Vienna School of Applied Arts from 1899 to 1937, Hoffmann, along with Viennese architect Kolo Moser, opened the Wiener Werkstätte, a workshop that produced furniture, leatherworks, and metalworks, today considered modern antiques.

Hoffmann's most famous work is the Palais Stocklet in Brussels, a house he codesigned with artists such as Gustav Klimt and which has been called "a work of such maturity and artistic grandeur as had not originated in Europe since the days of the Baroque."

245. *Hoffmann Rocking Chair.* Adjustable rocking chair. Beech bentwood; caned seat and back. 28¾ x 50½ x 45½″. Wittmann

246. *Purkersdorf.* Chair. 1903. Wooden frame with white high-gloss finish, spanned with black-and-white straps; a loose cushion serves as backrest. 24 x 24 x 33″. Wittmann

247. Chair. Wood, upholstered with fabric. Thonet (West Germany)

248. *Kubus.* Armchair. 1910. Construction on black socles with semispherical cups; upholstered in leather. 36 x 30½ x 28½″. Two- and three-seat sofa also available. Wittmann

249. *Armlöffel.* Dining-room chair. 1908. Chalked ebonized ash with loose cushion. 25¾ x 19⅞ x 37½″. Wittmann

250. *Cabinett.* Armchair. Linear dark-stained wooden frame with fabric covering. 47½ x 18 x 18½″. Wittmann

251. *Cabinett.* Table. Cubic dark-stained wooden frame; circular marble top. 34 x 34 x 24⅜″. Wittmann

252. *Fledermaus.* Table. Bentwood frame; top covered with fabric. Diameter 25¾″; height 25⅜″. Wittmann

253. *Purkersdorf.* Table. 1903. Wood with white high-gloss finish. 27½ x 27½ x 28½″. Wittmann

254. *Fledermaus.* Chair. Bentwood frame; upholstered seat and back covered with fabric. 19½ x 18 x 30″. Settee also available. Wittmann

255. *Villa Gallia.* Armchair and two-seat sofa. 1913. Wooden frame; upholstered and covered with unicolor fabric. Wittmann

256. *Haus Koller.* Armchair. 1911. Wooden frame; upholstered and covered with unicolor fabric. 35½ x 32 x 37". Two- and three-seat sofa also available. Wittmann

257. Table centerpiece. Silver 800. Rossi & Arcandi

258. *Form 15.* Mokka service. China, available in plain color or with stripes. Augarten

259. *Villa Spitzer.* Table lamp. Diameter 9⅜"; height 15⅜". Woka

260. *Villa Spitzer.* Ceiling lamp. Diameter 10½"; height 8⅛". Woka

261. *Villa Spitzer.* Ceiling lamp. Diameter 10½"; height 4⅝". Woka

262. Floor lamp. Diameter 19½"; height 70⅜". Woka

263. Floor lamp. Diameter 19½"; height 62⅜". Woka

264. Appliqué lamp. Diameter 7⅞"; height 17½". Woka

265. *Purkersdorf.* Appliqué lamp. Depth 11⅜"; height 23⅜". Woka

266. Appliqué lamp. Width 9¾"; height 19½". Woka

267. Appliqué lamp. Woka

268. Set of objets. Round fruit bowl; square flower pot holder; hexagonal vase; candy/sugar container; two-part fruit bowl; fruit basket; square wastepaper basket; hexagonal umbrella stand. Bieffeplast

269. Table lamp. Depth 11⅛"; height 23⅜". Woka

270. Table lamp. Width 4⅝"; height 19½". Woka

271. Appliqué lamp. Width 8⅝"; height 11¾". Woka

272. Appliqué lamp. Width 11¾"; height 8⅝". Woka

273. Nesting tables. 1905. Solid natural or black-stained ash. Largest to smallest: 19¾ x 16 x 27½"; 17 x 14⅝ x 26⅛"; 14¼ x 13¼ x 24¾"; 11½ x 11⅞ x 23⅜". ICF (U.S.)

274. *Orlik.* Fabric. 1908. Viscose and cotton. Bachausen

275. *Bienenkorb.* Fabric. 1902. Polyacryl and cotton. Bachausen

276. *Matisse.* Fabric. 1908. Viscose and cotton. Bachausen

277. *Zickzack.* Fabric. Viscose and cotton. Bachausen

278. *Notschrei.* Fabric. Gray, black, or gold; cotton and vicuna. Wittmann

279. *Aristide.* Fabric. Blue, red, or green; cotton and viscose. (This fabric is credited to Professor Otto Prutscher in the Bachausen catalogue.) Wittmann

280. *Inka.* Fabric. Cotton and polyester. Wittmann

281. Armchair. 1929. Steam-bent wood elm frame. 19¾ x 20¾ x 31½". Thonet (U.S.)

282. Side chair. 1929. Steam-bent wood elm frame. 17½ x 20¾ x 31½". Thonet (U.S.)

283. *Fledermaus.* Chair. 1905. Steam-bent American elm frame; seat upholstered with recessed welt over steel springs and fabric straps; rubberized fiber pad and urethane foam. 22½ x 18 x 29½". Thonet (U.S.)

284. *Fledermaus.* Table. 1905. Steam-bent American elm frame with round or square top (brass trim on base optional); inset top covered with vinyl, leather, genuine marble, or plastic laminate. Diameter 24"; height 30". Thonet (U.S.)

Hans Hollein (b. 1934)

Born and trained in Vienna, Hans Hollein was among those who, in the early 1960s, questioned the tenets of modern functionalism and expressed through his elegant sketches and photomontages how architecture could be approached differently. Hollein's controversial remodeling of the tiny Retti Candle Shop in Vienna shocked the architectural community with its reinterpretation of functionalism and its mixture of clever and sophisticated aesthetic complexities. Hollein has also designed with equal technical skill a gallery in New York, shops in Vienna, exhibition designs, and two museums in Germany.

285. Fruit bowl. Silver. Rossi & Arcandi

286. Candelabra. Silver. 17⅛ x 4⅝ x 12". Rossi & Arcandi

287. Fruit bowl. Silver. Diameter 17½"; height 7⅞". Rossi & Arcandi

288. *Zauberflote.* Dressing table. Acrylic glass with ostrich feathers. 96⅝ x 19½ x 78". Möbel Industrie Design

208

210

209

211

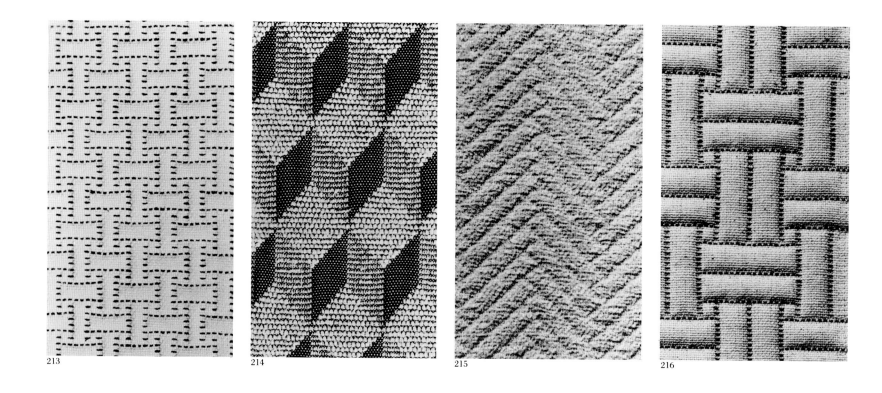

213

214

215

216

219-224

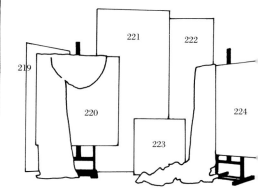

219

220

221

222

223

224

217

218

225

228

226

227

229

225–229

230

231

232–237

138

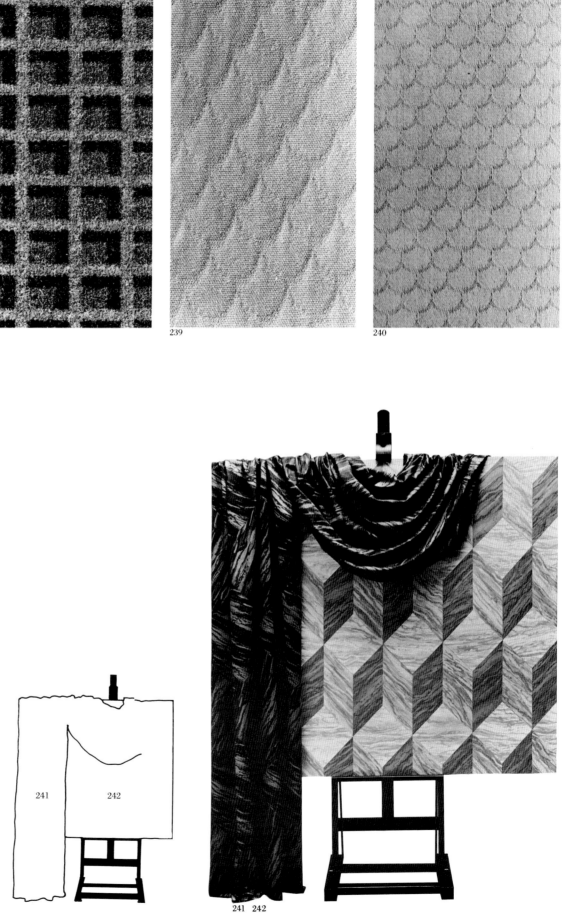

238

239

240

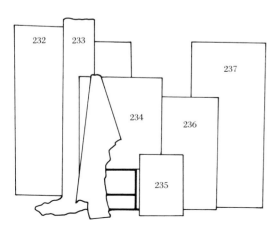

232 233

237

234

236

235

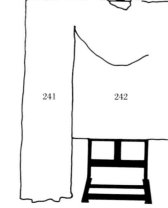

241 242

241 242

243

244

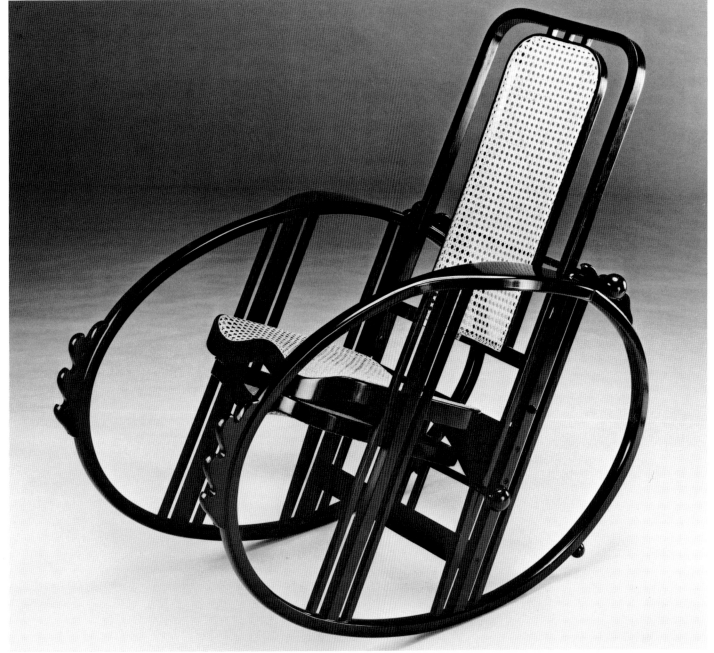

245

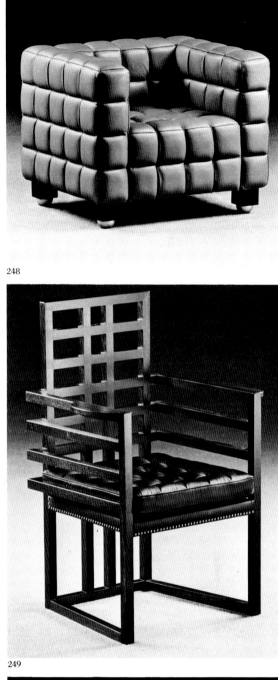

248

249

246

247

250

251

252

253

254

255

256

257

258

259

260

261

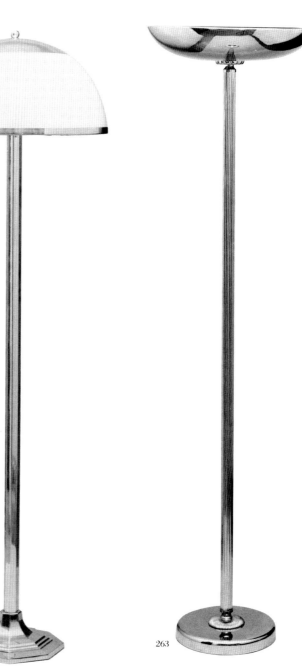

262

263

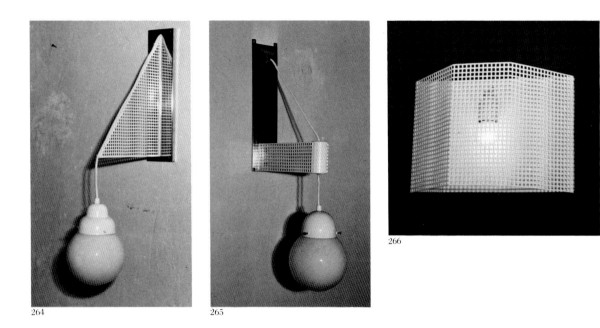

264

265

266

267

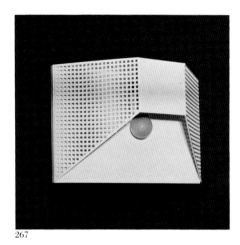

268

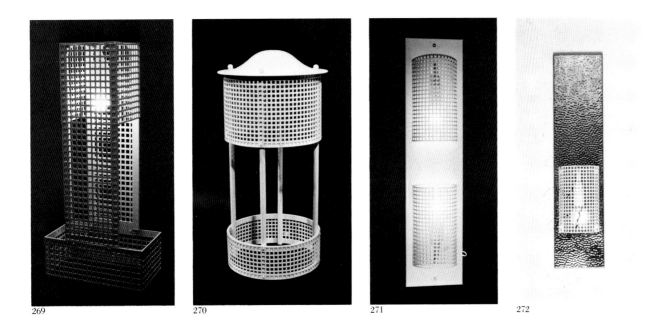

269 270 271 272

273

274

275

276

277

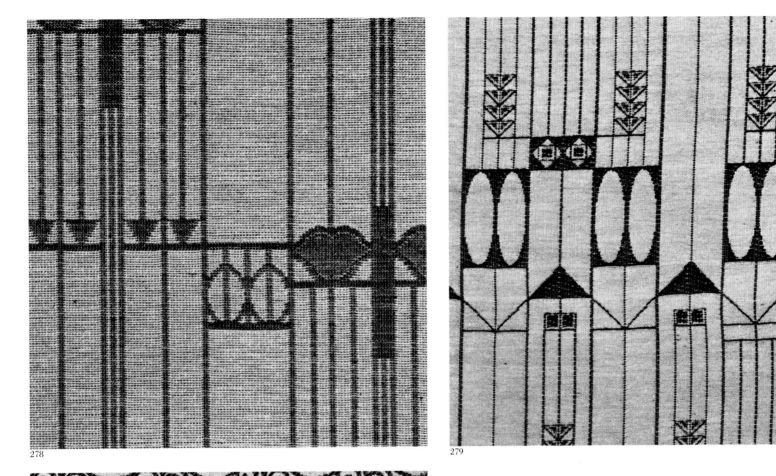

278

279

280

281

282

283 284

285

286

287

288

154

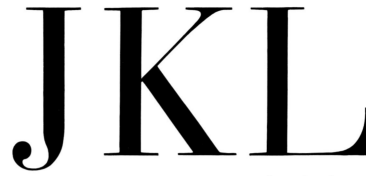

JKL

Arne Jacobsen

Kaare Klint

Kisho Kurokawa

El Lissitzky

Adolf Loos

Arne Jacobsen (1902–1971)

The most outstanding Danish architect of the twentieth century, Arne Jacobsen designed buildings and furniture that combined the best techniques of the industrial world with the finest materials and craftsmanship. His personal talent for designing simple but sophisticated spaces and his ability for finding solutions led him to design many buildings in Denmark and abroad, his most famous being the SAS Royal Hotel in Copenhagen. In this one building he designed everything down to the hotel's cutlery.

Jacobsen's bentwood metal-legged chair from the early 1950s continues to be a classic bestseller.

289. *The Swan.* Armchair. 1959. Shell in molded polyurethane reinforced with fiberglass on which is glued molded latex; upholstered in leather, fabric, or vinyl; starbase in cast-polished aluminum with a column in chromed steel. 29 x 27 x 29½″. Fritz Hansen

290. *The Egg.* Armchair. 1959. Shell in model polyurethane reinforced with fiberglass on which is glued molded latex; upholstered in leather, fabric, or vinyl; starbase in cast-polished aluminum with a column in chromed steel; equipped with loose seat cushion. 34 x 31 x 42″. Ottoman also available. Fritz Hansen

291. *Oxford.* Chair with or without armrests. Swiveling starbase in cast aluminum; seat and back of molded laminated wood; upholstery glued to seat and back, in molded foam; arm bracket in cast aluminum. Width 18⅜–24⅞″; depth 21″; height 35⅛–53″. Fritz Hansen

292a–f. *Serie 7.* Chair. 1955. Seat and back shell made of molded plywood, with or without padding; chromium-plated steel tubing base; stained finishes on beech or teak or eight colors lacquered finish; several models available. Dimensions vary according to style. Fritz Hansen

293. Chair. 1952. Shell in molded plywood; chromed tubular steel base; available in eight colors with lacquered finish. Fritz Hansen

294. Chair. Shell in molded plywood; chromed tubular steel base; available in natural beech, natural teak, or in color. Fritz Hansen

295a–d. Table. Square, rectangular, circular, and elliptical tops in composite board, white plastic laminate with matt-polished edge, natural beech with solid edge, wengé stained with solid edge, stained teak or natural teak with solid teak edge; shaker in aluminum with column in chrome steel; tubular legs in chrome. Dimensions vary according to style. Fritz Hansen

296. *Cylinda Line.* Coffeepot, creamer, sugar bowl with lid, serving tray. 1966. Stainless steel, synthetic coffeepot handle. Stelton

297. *Cylinda Line.* Teapot, hot-water jug, milk jug, jam pot, tea streamer with bowl, toast rack. 1966. Stainless steel. Stelton

298. *Cylinda Line.* Salt and pepper set, salt and pepper shakers and mustard pot on tray, pepper mill, butter sauciere, sauce server. 1966. Stainless steel. Stelton

299. *Cylinda Line.* Salad/fruit bowl, salad servers, pepper mill and salt shaker. 1966. Stainless steel. Stelton

300. *Cylinda Line.* Pitchers. 1966. Stainless steel. Stelton

301. *Cylinda Line.* Serving dishes. 1966. Stainless steel. Stelton

302. *Cylinda Line.* Ice buckets, martini set with strainer and mixer spoon, ice tongs, ashtray, coasters. 1966. Stainless steel. Stelton

303. *Cylinda Line.* Wine cooler/ice bucket, cocktail shaker, ashtray. 1966. Stainless steel. Stelton

304. Stainless steel cutlery. 1957. Knives forged in knife steel, other items in cold pressed steel. A. Michelsen

305. *A. J. Pendant.* Hanging lamp. Metal shade in dark or light gray, dark brown, or white; three 60-watt bulbs. Diameter 19¼″; height 8⅞″. Louis Poulsen

306/307. *A. J. Ceiling and Wall Lamp.* Wall and ceiling lamp. White metal holder, opal glass; wall lamp, 40-watt bulb; ceiling lamp, 60-watt bulb. Wall lamp diameter 8⅞″, height 4½″; ceiling lamp diameter 13⅝″, height 3⅞″. Louis Poulsen

308. *Munkegaard Lamp.* Ceiling lamp. White-lacquered metal housing; matt brass or chromium-plated rim; opal glass plate; 60-watt bulb. Diameter 9¾″. Louis Poulsen

309. Floor and table lamp. Steel; 60-watt bulb. Diameter 6″; height 50⅞″, 21″. Louis Poulsen

310. *A. J. Park Lamp.* Park lamp. Shade of opal synthetic material; metal parts of hot galvanized iron; 100-watt incandescent bulb. Diameter 31¼″. Louis Poulsen

311a–b. *Vola.* Kitchen or bathroom mixers. Brass and copper. I. P. Lund

Kaare Klint (b. 1888)

A Danish architect and director of the furniture school at the Royal Danish Academy, Kaare Klint was the son of the master-builder Peter Klint. For his Bethlehem Church in Copenhagen, Kaare Klint designed all the details, including the stamps used on the envelopes for the church opening's invitations. Klint also worked with textile design. His geometric patterns and use of natural colors have been called elements of the "Klint School."

312. *Frugtlygte.* Hanging lamp. Handmade lampshade; 75-watt bulb. Diameter 10½"; height 14". Le Klint

313. *Kliplampe.* Wall lamp. Base in brass; handmade lampshade; 75-watt bulb. Diameter 8¼"; height 15⅝". Le Klint

314. *Kliplampe.* Table lamp. Stainless steel with brass base and fittings; handmade lampshade; 40- or 60-watt bulb. Diameter 8¼"; height 29⅝". Le Klint

315. *The Ladder Back Chair.* Armless chair. Oak finish with matt lacquer; woven paper-cord seat. 20¼ x 19½ x 32¾". Fritz Hansen

Kisho Kurokawa (b. 1934)

A member of the Japanese Metabolist group who, in the mid-1950s, challenged the old modern Japanese architectural masters, Kisho Kurokawa has demonstrated through his buildings how technological developments can be applied to architecture. His High-Tech Pavilion at Expo '70, his Nakagin Capsule Building in Tokyo, and the Osaka Sony Tower are examples of this application. His present architectural commissions include buildings in Hungary, West Germany, and the Middle East.

316. *Serie Edo.* High back chair. Lacquer finish; seat covered with leather. 17⅛ x 19½ x 54⅝". Kosuga & Co.

317. *Serie Edo.* Coffee table. Plate in pair glass; legs in matt urethane paint finish. 35⅛ x 35⅛ x 12⅞". Kosuga & Co.

318. *Serie Edo.* Dining-room chair. Matt urethane paint finish; cloth-covered seat. 16⅜ x 19⅛ x 37⅞". Kosuga & Co.

319. *Serie Edo.* Large dining table. Top in pair glass; legs in matt urethane paint finish. 70⅞ x 35⅝ x 27". Kosuga & Co.

320. *Serie Edo.* Small dining table. Top in pair glass with Japanese handmade paper in between; legs in matt urethane paint finish. 31¼ x 31¼ x 27". Kosuga & Co.

321. *Serie Edo.* Armchair. Matt urethane paint finish; cloth-covered cushion. 25¾ x 25¾ x 25⅜". Kosuga & Co.

El Lissitzky (1890–1941)

One of Constructivism's cofounders, El Lissitzky, the Russian architect, held several official and semi-official positions in the U.S.S.R., among them the directorship of the Moscow architectural faculty and the directorship of architectural works in Moscow's Gorki Park. His interests also included the graphic arts, which led to his designing of many books.

322. Armchair. 1930. Plexiglas. Tecta

Adolf Loos (1870–1933)

One of modern architecture's pioneers and the author of the influential essay "Ornament and Crime," the Austrian architect and theorist Adolf Loos devoted a lifetime to freeing architecture from "superficial decoration." Loos believed that anything that could not be justified on rational grounds was superfluous, a belief he translated into his puritan buildings, houses, and interior designs. Among the best known are his Steiner House in Vienna and the Tristan Tzara House in Paris. Loos's philosophies eventually paved the way for the aesthetic questions raised by the Bauhaus.

323. Crystal glass service. J & L Lobmeyr

324. *Villa Steiner Serie.* Table lamp. Diameter 13⅝"; height 25⅜". Woka

325. *Villa Steiner Serie.* Table lamp. Diameter 9¾–11¾"; height 5⅞". Woka

326. *Villa Steiner Serie.* Floor lamp. Diameter 19½"; height 62⅜". Woka

290

291

292 a   292 b   292 c

293

294

292d

292e

292f

295 a

295 b

295 c

295 d

296

297

298

299

300

301

302

303

304

305

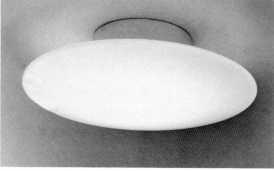

306

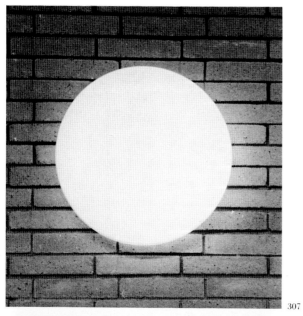

307

308

309

310

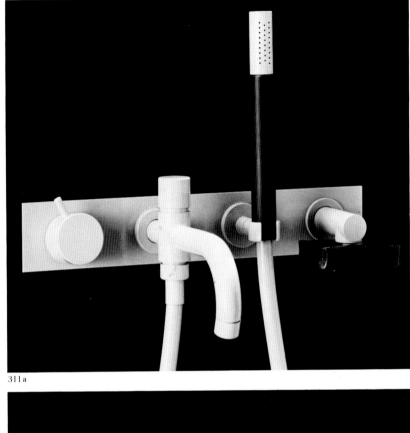

311a

311b

312

313

314

315

316

317

318

319

320

321

322

323

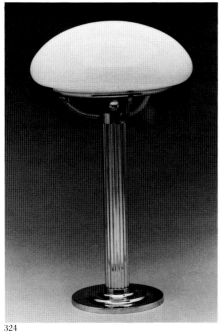

324

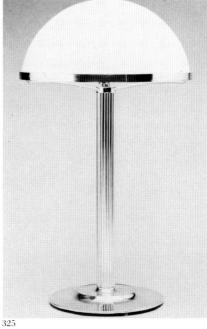

325

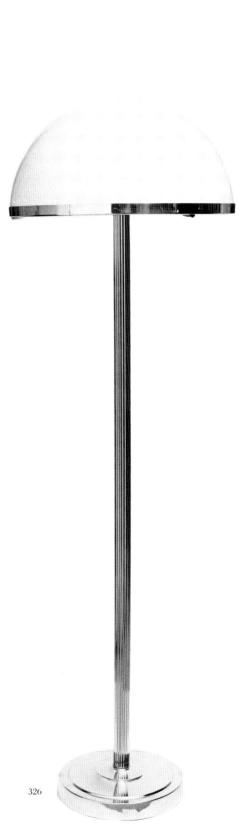

326

Charles Rennie Mackintosh

Robert Mallet-Stevens

Angelo Mangiarotti

Vittorio Mazzuconni

Richard Meier

Roberto Menghi

Ludwig Mies van der Rohe

Koloman Moser

Leonardo Mosso

Charles Rennie Mackintosh (1868–1928)

A leading figure in the Art Nouveau movement in Great Britain, Charles Rennie Mackintosh attended the Glasgow School of Art (for which he later built extensions) and through it formed a group called The Four. The Four consisted of Mackintosh, Herbert MacNair, and Frances and Margaret Macdonald, and together they invented a bold new approach to interior design practices. In 1900 he and his wife, Margaret Macdonald, designed a tea room for the Vienna Secessionist Exhibition. It caused a sensation and established Mackintosh as a leading architect.

Mackintosh was also interested in furniture design and based its elegant forms on the right angle and straight line. In 1913 he limited his practice to furniture and fabric design and a few years later retired and devoted himself to watercolor painting and the study of nature.

327. *Hill House I*. Ladder-back chair. 1902–3. Ebonized ashwood frame; seat upholstered in special fabric, green on pink. 16 x 15¼ x 55". Cassina

328. *Argyle*. Chair. 1897. Ebonized ashwood frame; seat upholstered in special fabric, blue. 18¾ x 17⅞ x 53". Cassina

329. *D.S.2*. Table. 1918. Ebonized ashwood frame. 29¼ x 29¼ x 29¼". Cassina

330. *D.S.3*. Side chair. 1918. Ebonized ashwood frame inlaid with mother-of-pearl; sea-grass seat. 19⅛ x 17½ x 29¼". Cassina

331. *D.S.4*. Lounge chair. 1918. Ebonized ashwood frame inlaid with mother-of-pearl; sea-grass seat. 20¼ x 17½ x 29¼". Cassina

332. *D.S.1*. Table. 1918. Ebonized ashwood frame; folding top at two sides. 69 x 48¾ x 29¼". Cassina

333. *Willow I*. Curved lattice-back chair. 1904. Ebonized ashwood frame; seat cushion upholstered in special fabric, beige or green. 36 ⅝ x 16 x 46⅜". Cassina

334. *Willow 2*. Chair. Ebonized ashwood frame; sea-grass seat. 15⅞ x 15¼ x 54⅞". Cassina

335. *D.S.5*. Cupboard. 1918. Ebonized ashwood frame; colored glass mosaic decoration bound with lead and inlaid with mother-of-pearl. 63½ x 22¼ x 58⅞". Cassina

336. *Glasgow School of Art. (G.S.A)*. Table. 1900. Ash-stained walnut frame; veneer top in ash-stained walnut with revolving central part. Diameter 74⅛"; height 28⅞". Cassina

337. Tea table. 1911. Black-stained and varnished oak. 30¼ x 19½ x 19½". B. D. Ediciones

338. *Ingram, High*. High-back chair. 1900. Solid ash-stained walnut frame; cushion padding in polyurethane foam and Dacron; upholstered in exclusive fabric. 18⅞ x 17⅜ x 58½". Low-back version also available. Cassina

339. Chair. 1903. Silver-painted oak; upper seat back inlaid with purple-colored glass; seat and back upholstered with lilac velvet. 52⅝ x 19⅛ x 18¾". B. D. Ediciones

340. Square table. 1903. Silver-painted wood; legs inlaid with purple-colored glass. 28½ x 28½ x 28⅝". B. D. Ediciones

341. Coat and umbrella stand. Silver-painted mahogany; hanger and umbrella holders in blackened iron; drip-pans in silver-plated brass. Diameter 11⅞"; height 78". B. D. Ediciones

342. Writing desk. 1904. Black-stained and varnished mahogany with sycamore; mother-of-pearl and ivory incrustations; base inlaid with lilac-colored glass; ornamental interior panel decorated with metal. 47¼ x 36⅝ x 18⅜". B. D. Ediciones

343. Candlesticks. 1904. Black-stained and varnished sycamore with or without incrustations of mother-of-pearl; silver fixing ring and pan. 12 x 5⅞ x 16⅜". B. D. Ediciones

344. Chair. 1904. Black-stained and varnished sycamore; seat upholstered in white linen. 43⅜ x 15⅞ x 18⅝". B. D. Ediciones

345. Large and small carpets. 1903. Woven wool in white, green, red, and lilac. Small carpet 58⅛ x 35½"; large carpet 58⅛ x 58⅛". B. D. Ediciones

346. Table. 1903. Black-stained and varnished sycamore; base and top inlaid with mother-of-pearl. 24⅛ x 27¾ x 26¾". B. D. Ediciones

347. Armchair. 1917. Stained and varnished oak; back inlaid with mother-of-pearl; spring seat and cushioned arm upholstered with blue, green, gray, or red linen velvet. 29¾ x 32¼ x 26¼". B. D. Ediciones

348. Chair. 1911. Black-stained and varnished sycamore; upholstered seat. 32⅛ x 17⅛ x 15⅞". B. D. Ediciones

349. *Argyle Set*. Armchair and settee. Stained walnut on ebonized ashwood frame; polyurethane foam and polyester fiber padding; upholstered in exclusive fabric. Armchair 26⅛ x 26⅛ x 27⅜"; settee 45⅝ x 26⅛ x 27⅜". Sofa also available. Cassina

Robert Mallet-Stevens (1886–1945)

In the 1920s and 1930s, Robert Mallet-Stevens was the most successful of the French modernist architects. He achieved this reputation through his designing of a variety of buildings, houses, shops, and film sets. For his important commissions, Mallet-Stevens often formed working teams and through them collaborated with people such as Van Doesburg, Léger, and Robert Delaunay.

350. Dining chair. Lacquered metal; upholstered cushion available. Ecart International/Pallucco

Angelo Mangiarotti (b. 1921)

Long interested in building techniques and prefabrication methods, Angelo Mangiarotti is considered one of the most romantic Italian architects and furniture designers. His thoughts on man and the environment and his perception of architecture as a total art are reflected in the fluid and formal language of his architecture and in the refined, simple statements of his industrial designs.

351. *De Nos Serie.* High and low chair. Walnut frame and upholstery. High chair 17½ x 19⅞ x 30"; low chair 17½ x 19⅞ x 38⅝". Arcani/Skipper

352. *De Nos Serie.* Triangular or square stool. Walnut frame and upholstery. Square 17 x 17 x 16"; rectangular 18 x 18 x 16". Arcani/Skipper

353. *De Nos Serie.* Table series. 1974–80. Walnut frame and glass top. Dimensions vary according to style. Arcani/Skipper

354. *De Nos Serie.* Bed. Walnut frame, mattress, and upholstery. 71¾ x 85½ x 38⅝". Single bed also available. Arcani/Skipper

355. *De Nos Serie.* Vitrine. Walnut frame and glass. 21⅞ x 37½ x 69". Arcani/Skipper

356. *3 Tre.* Chair. 1977–78. Solid walnut frame; seat natural leather and steel. 21½ x 22¼ x 26⅛". Arcani/Skipper

357. *Eros E Fiorera.* 1971. Multiform table. Top and legs in La Versilia marble. Dimensions vary according to style. Fucina/Skipper

358. High or low rectangular or square tables. Top and legs in La Versilia marble. Dimensions vary according to style. Fucina/Skipper

359. *Incas.* High or low round or elliptical tables. Base in bronze casting; top in marble. Dimensions vary according to style. G. B. Bernini

360. *Asolo.* Square, round, or rectangular tables. Black or red granite. Dimensions vary according to style. Fucina/Skipper

361. *Isomix.* Bathroom mixer. Stella

362. Triangular flower vases. Silver 800. Rossi & Arcandi

363. Water pitcher and drinking glasses. Silver 800. Rossi & Arcandi

364. *Stradivarius.* System shelves. Wood. Available in varying widths, depths, and heights. Apotem

365. Flower pots. White marble. Horus-Skipper

366. Flower pots. Bronze. Horus-Skipper

367. Flower pots. 1971. Marble. Horus-Skipper

368. *Central Park.* Table and stools. Marble and glass. Arcani/Skipper

369. *Alola.* Floor lamp with adjustable reflector. Pressed polycarbonate enameled in black or white; stem finish in chrome; 250-watt halogen bulb. 12⅞ x 14 x 78". Table and wall lamp also available. Pollux/Skipper

370. *Lesbo.* Table lamp. Aluminum; 75-watt bulb. Diameter 20¼"; height 14⅜". Artemide

371. *Egina Sospensione.* Hanging lamp. White or transparent glass. Diameters 10⅞–14⅞". Artemide

372. *Lari.* Table lamp. Glass; two 75-watt bulbs. 16⅞ x 6⅝ x 14⅜". Artemide

373. *Saffo.* Table lamp. Aluminum; 40-watt bulb. Diameter 8¼"; height 12⅞". Artemide

374. *Strozzi.* Hanging lamp. Chromed brass and glass. Depth 27⅜"; height 39". Candle

375. *Cavea.* Outdoor lamp. Glass and aluminum. Height 8⅞". Artemide

376. *Cerbero.* Outdoor lamp. Glass and aluminum. Heights 58½", 97½". Artemide

377. *Cementa.* Outdoor lamp. Cement; pressed glass; aluminum casting. 12⅞ x 15¼ x 27⅝". Candle

Vittorio Mazzuconni (b. 1940)

For the Italian architect Vittorio Mazzuconni, architecture is neither a purely functionalist practice nor a decorative art but a discipline involving human, psychological, social, and spatial experiences. This philosophical approach has resulted in his designing bold and formal projects based on an original and highly personalized architectural language.

378. *Positiv.* Two-seat sofa. Base in Plexiglas; upholstered in leather. ICF (Italy) and Formes nouvelles

Richard Meier (b. 1934)

The American architect Richard Meier has written that his architecture is "an attempt to clarify and refine a sense of order within society, to understand a relationship between what has been and what can be." Meier's international reputation was established with his designing of single-family residences, housing complexes, and commercial and industrial buildings such as the Bronx Psychiatric Center Warehouse in New York and the Atheneum in New Harmony, Indiana. His white organic buildings are often considered reminiscent of the International Style and his well-designed projects and elegantly proportioned architecture perceived as statements on spatial order and aesthetics.

379. Chair. 1982. Laminated hard maple veneer and solid hard maple frame; black and white finishes, hand-rubbed lacquer-urethane; natural finish, hand-rubbed low sheen vinyl. 21 x 20 x 27½". Knoll International

380. Table. 1982. Solid hard maple base; laminated hard maple veneer top; black and white finishes, hand-rubbed lacquer-urethane; natural finish, hand-rubbed low sheen vinyl. 60 x 96 x 27½". Knoll International

381. Table. 1982. Solid hard maple base; laminated hard maple veneer top; black and white finishes, hand-rubbed lacquer-urethane; natural finish, hand-rubbed low sheen vinyl. 40 x 40 x 15¼". Knoll International

382. Chaise. 1982. Channel-tufted cushion; down pillow; laminated hard maple veneer and solid hard maple frame; black and white finishes, hand-rubbed lacquer-urethane; natural finish, hand-rubbed low sheen vinyl. 72 x 27½ x 25⅛". Knoll International

383. Low stool. 1982. Laminated hard maple veneer and solid hard maple frame; black and white finishes, hand-rubbed lacquer-urethane; natural finish, hand-rubbed low sheen vinyl. Diameter 17⅝"; height 15¼". Knoll International

384. High stool. 1982. Laminated hard maple veneer and solid hard maple frame; cast stainless steel footring; black and white finish, hand-rubbed lacquer-urethane; natural finish, hand-rubbed low sheen vinyl. Diameter 15⅜"; height 27½". Knoll International

Roberto Menghi (b. 1920)

In the 1950s and 1960s a variety of projects by the Italian architect Roberto Menghi were published in numerous architectural magazines. Menghi's buildings are remarkable for their intelligent handling of space and their clever use of modern materials, among them the Piazza St. Ambrogio in Italy.

385. *Safari.* Dismountable armchair. 1976. Bay oak, natural color; tilting back; removable headrest; covering of Canapone or "Tela Strong," removable. Zanotta

Ludwig Mies van der Rohe (1886–1969)

The master of the modern movement and the practitioner of the philosophy "Less is more," Ludwig Mies van der Rohe was born in Germany, the son of a stonecutter. Although he did not receive formal training in architecture, his apprenticeships with Bruno Paul (the furniture designer) and Peter Behrens provided him with an invaluable education. Within three years of his apprenticeships, he opened his own firm.

After the war, Mies designed several spectacular projects, among them two glass skyscrapers with cantilevered floors (he would later become the master of steel and glass) that became prototypes for a building he realized thirty years later on the shores of Lake Michigan. His commission to design the German Pavilion at the Barcelona Fair in 1929 allowed him to apply his own concepts of an open plan with free-standing walls and fluid space. The Pavilion was hailed as a masterpiece.

In 1930 Mies was appointed director of the Bauhaus but closed down the school three years later as a gesture against Nazism. Afterward he moved to Chicago, where he took over the direction of the School of Architecture at the Illinois Institute of Technology, a chairmanship he held for twenty years.

Among his best-known works were those realized in the United States: the Lake Shore Drive Apartments in Chicago; the Farnsworth House in Plano, Illinois; Crown Hall at the Illinois Institute; and the Seagram Building in New York.

386. *Brno Armchair.* Armchair. 1929–30. Frame in flat stainless steel with polished finish; constructed hardwood seat and back frame; foam over spring suspension for seat; foam over sagless burlap for back. 23 x 23 x 31½″. Knoll International

387. *Barcelona Table.* Low table. 1929. Stainless steel base; polished plate-glass top. 40 x 40 x 17″. Knoll International

388. *Barcelona Stool.* Stool. 1929. Frame in stainless steel with polished finish; foam mattress with polyester fiber padding covered with leather. 23 x 22 x 14¼″. Knoll International

389. *Barcelona Chair.* Chair. 1929. Frame in stainless steel with polished finish; foam mattress with polyester fiber padding covered with leather. 30 x 30 x 30″. Knoll International

390a–b. *Mr Chair.* Chair (with or without arms). 1927. Frame in tubular stainless steel with polished finish; upholstered in saddle leather sling with nylon lacing. Armless 19½ x 27¼ x 31″; with arms 21 x 32½ x 31″. Knoll International

391. *Brno Chair.* Chair. 1929–30. Frame in tubular stainless steel with polished finish; constructed hardwood seat and back frame; foam over spring suspension for seat; foam over sagless burlap for back. 22 x 23¼ x 32½″. Knoll International

392. Adjustable chaise lounge. 1931. Frame in tubular stainless steel with polished finish; foam cushions covered with fabric or leather. 26 x 70¼ x 30½–35¼″. Knoll International

393. Lounge chair with arms. 1931. Frame in tubular stainless steel with polished finish; foam cushions covered in fabric or leather. 23⅝ x 36¼ x 33″. Knoll International

394a–b. *Mr Chair.* Chair with or without arms. 1927. Steel tubular frame with polished finish; seat and back in leather or wickwork. 19½ x 29¼ x 31⅞″. Thonet (West Germany)

395. Chaise lounge. 1931. Frame in tubular stainless steel with polished finish; foam cushions covered with fabric or leather. 23⅝ x 47¼ x 37½″. Knoll International

396. Occasional table. Smoked-plate glass top; tubular stainless steel base. Diameter 27½″; height 19⅝″. Knoll International

397. Couch. Hardwood frame with saddle leather straps over rubber webbing; legs in tubular stainless steel polished finish; foam mattress with polyester fiber padding covered in leather. 78 x 39 x 15½″. Knoll International

Koloman (Kolo) Moser (1868–1918)

The Viennese architect Kolo Moser was the director, as well as one of the cofounders, of the famous studios and workshops known as the Weiner Werkstätte. It was there he designed his many objects and pieces of furniture.

398. Pendant. 1904. Diameter 13⅝″; length adjustable to 47″. Woka

399. Pendant. 1904. Diameter 19½″; length adjustable to 47″. Woka

400. Spot lamp. Diameter 6¼″; height 5⅞″. Woka

401. Table lamp. Diameter 8⅞″; height 17½″. Woka

402a–b. *Kolo Moser Fabric.* Fabric. Green/red or green/blue, in silk and cotton. Wittmann

Leonardo Mosso

A long-time assistant to Alvar Aalto, the Italian architect Leonardo Mosso supervised several of Aalto's construction projects.

403. Object. Silver and glass mirror. Rossi & Arcandi

327

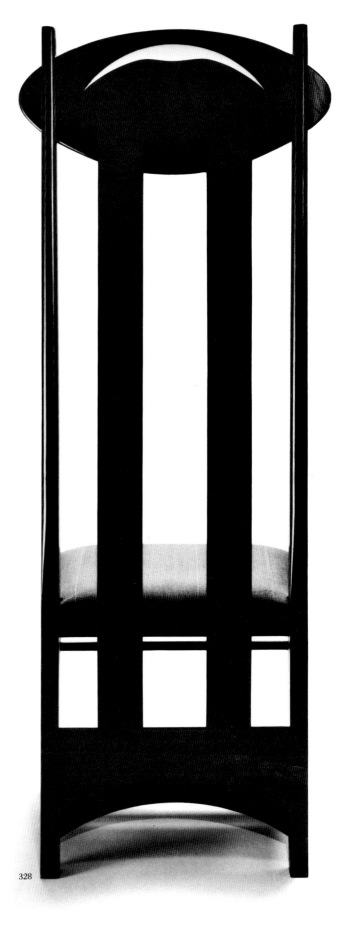

328

329

330

331

331 332

333

334

335

336

337

336 338

Mackintosh

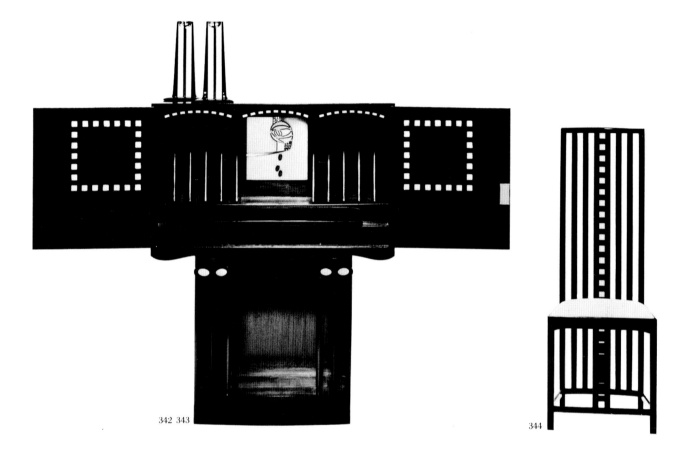

342 343

344

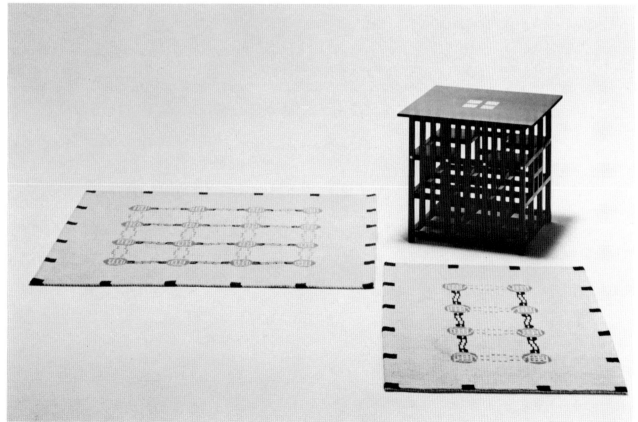

345 346

348

349

350

348

349

350

351 352

353

354

355

356

357

358

359

360

361

362

363

364

365

366

367

368

370

371

372

373

374

375

376

377

378

380

381

383

382

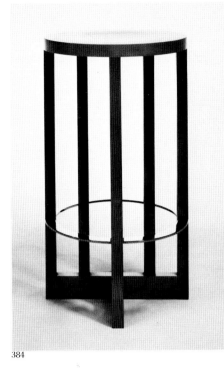

384

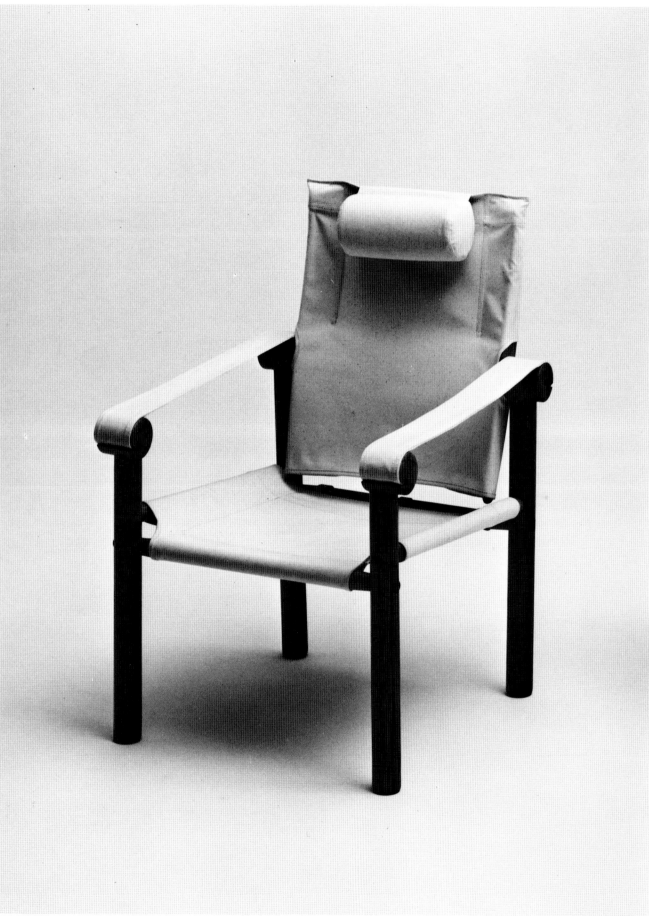

387

388

390 a

390 b

391

392

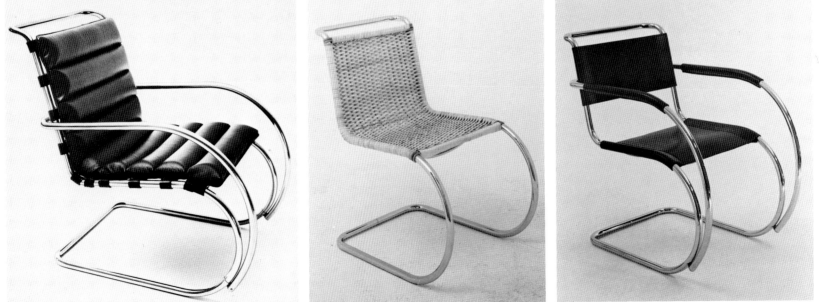

393   394a   394b

395

396

397

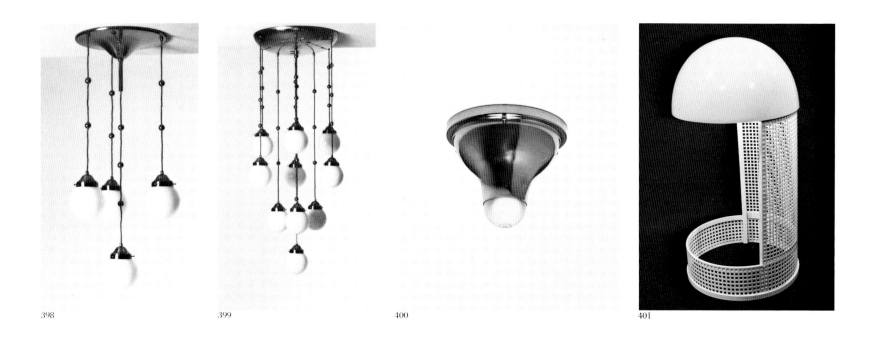

398

399

400

401

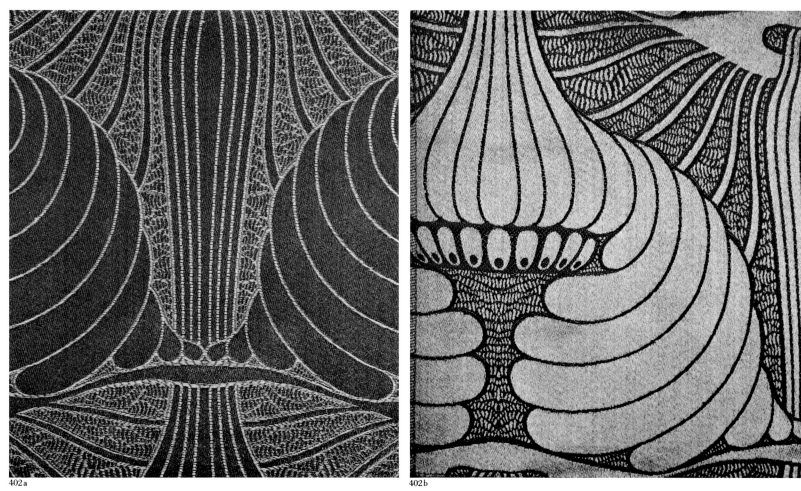

402 a

402 b

403

NOP

George Nelson

Oscar Niemeyer

Jacobus Johannes Pieter Oud

Studio PER

Charlotte Perriand

Gaetano Pesce

Warren Platner

Gio Ponti

Anna Praun

George Nelson (b. 1908)

Although he was trained as an architect, the American George Nelson started his professional practice as a journalist in the architectural press, and in 1943 became coeditor of Architectural Forum. *However, when two of his architectural projects—a storage wall unit and a preformed one-wall kitchen—caught the attention of the young but innovative firm Herman Miller, Nelson joined the company as its design director and later attracted furniture designers to the firm such as Charles Eames.*

Nelson has also designed several exhibitions, the most famous of them being the 1959 American National Exhibition in Moscow, and has written influential books on design.

404. *CSS.* Shelf system. Aluminum frame; shelves and cabinet in black ashwood. Shelves system-supporting structure, shelves, and cabinets available in varying widths, depths, and heights. Mobilier International

405. Sling sofa. 1964. Polished chrome-plated frame and base; seat and back cushions upholstered in top-grain leather; cushions of soft urethane foam enclosed by polyester fiber batting, supported by fabric-reinforced rubber webbing at back and neoprene platforms across seating area. 87 x 32¼ x 29¾". Herman Miller

Oscar Niemeyer (b. 1907)

The Brazilian architect Oscar Niemeyer invented his own architectural language with a group of public buildings he designed at Pampulha in the early 1940s and with his government buildings in Brasilia. Influenced, as many young South American architects were, by Le Corbusier's ideas and theories, Niemeyer was part of the team who, during the war, designed the Educational Ministry in Rio, a building where most of the characteristic features of modern Brazilian architecture were clearly expressed. Niemeyer's buildings are characterized by their light, floating quality.

406. Easy chair. Curved lumber; seat and back cushions covered with brown or black leather. 27½ x 41 x 28½". Tendo Brasileira

407. Low easy chair. Curved lumber; seat and back cushions covered with brown leather. 27½ x 44⅛ x 20⅛". Tendo Brasileira

408. Low easy chair. Curved lumber; seat and back cushions covered with brown or black leather. 27½ x 41⅛ x 21⅞". Tendo Brasileira

409. Low ottoman. Curved lumber; cushion covered with brown or black leather. 27½ x 27½ x 10". Tendo Brasileira

410. Low ottoman. Curved lumber; cushion covered with brown leather. 27½ x 28½ x 8⅝". Tendo Brasileira

411. High stool. Curved lumber; cushion covered with brown or black leather. 27½ x 27½ x 16⅛". Tendo Brasileira

412. Side table. Curved black lumber. 74 x 19¾ x 9⅞". Tendo Brasileira

413. Couch. Curved lumber; upholstery covered with black leather. 23⅜ x 75¼ x 22½". Tendo Brasileira

414. Chaise lounge. Bent blackwood frame; caned seat. Tendo Brasileira

Jacobus Johannes Pieter Oud (1890–1963)

One of the founders and active members of the De Stijl movement, J. J. P. Oud was, like many Dutch architects of postwar Netherlands, influenced by Cubism, Mondrian, and by the early work of Frank Lloyd Wright. A long-time city architect for Rotterdam, Oud created original designs for low-cost and working-class housing (the Tusschendijken and the Oud Mathenesse Housing Estates among them), which were later used as models for many European urban developments. Oud believed in standardization and in mass production of housing but was never limited by the machine aesthetic of the 1920s and 1930s. In the latter years of his life he designed projects with a more formalized mannerism.

415. Dining-room set. Metal with blue lacquer finish; top and seat in black-finished wood. Ecart International/Pallucco

416. Stool. Metal with blue lacquer finish; top in black-finished wood. Ecart International/Pallucco

Studio PER

The Barcelona-based Studio PER (created in the early 1960s) is known for its avant-garde approach to architecture, an approach that has resulted in its designing a noticeable series of buildings in Barcelona and the well-known Belvedere Georgina house in Gerona, Spain. In addition to building projects, the members of the group also design furniture and objects.

417. *Tumbona Du-Champ* (L. Clotet and O. Tusquets). Chaise lounge. Structure in steel with stain; bicycle wheels; back and seat in expanded metal with white plastic paint, covering with nylon voile optional. Adjustable heights 28–70¼″. B. D. Ediciones

418. *Banco Catalano* (L. Clotet and O. Tusquets). Public bench. 1973. Steel structure; seat and back in expanded steel painted with white or green epoxy. Depth 19½″; height 34¾″. B. D. Ediciones

419. *Serie Rácor* (P. Bonet). Bathroom fixtures. 1976. Plastic or aluminum covered with plastic; black or white. Single bar, double bar, and shelf lengths 15⅝–46⅞″. Can be combined as shown in diagram. B. D. Ediciones

420a–c. *Herrajes B.D.* (C. Cirici). Door hardware (knob, handle, and pull). Anodized aluminum, bronze, or silver. B. D. Ediciones

421. *Carrito Versátil* (L. Clotet and O. Tusquets). Television trolley. Steel structure with castors. 20½–31¾ x 15⅛ x 25⅜″. B. D. Ediciones

422. *Estantería Hypóstila* (L. Clotet and O. Tusquets). Shelves for heavy weights. 1979. Anodized aluminum. Widths 78–156″; depths 5⅞–9¾″. B. D. Ediciones

423. *Galan de Baño* (P. Bonet). Bath valet. Wood with lacquer finish. 16¾ x 10⅞ x 46″. B. D. Ediciones

424. *Sevilla.* (P. Bonet, C. Cirici, and M. Riera). Table and chairs. Table structure in metal; top in painted glass, marble, laminated wood, or metalgrid; black or white. Chair structure in light metal; seat and back in acrylic canvas; black, white, blue, and beige. 27⅜ x 27⅜ x 28″. B. D. Ediciones

425. *Theo Walter* (P. Bonet). Record case. Black metal box with plasticized finish; sliding lids in metacrylate. B. D. Ediciones

426. *Mesa Burguesa* (A. Bohigas and L. Clotet). Sitting-room table. Black-lacquered wood and mahogany color-stained mapletree root veneer. 15½ x 31 x 15½″. B. D. Ediciones

427. *Buzones a Sardinel* (L. Clotet and O. Tusquets). Mail boxes. Matt or ivory metal plate; door of transparent metacrylate and stainless steel. Each box 3 x 11½ x 15½″. B. D. Ediciones

428. *Lámpara Consentida* (L. Clotet and O. Tusquets). Lift door lamp. Anodized aluminum extruded shape and grill; 20-watt fluorescent tube. Depth 4¼″; height 1⅞″. B. D. Ediciones

429. *Campana BD* (L. Clotet, O. Tusquets, and A. Bohigas). Kitchen extractor hood. Centrifugal extractor; transparent metacrylate hood; hot painted white metal plate; 13-watt fluorescent tube; flexible aluminum tube. 27⅜–35⅛ x 19½ x 16½″. B. D. Ediciones

Charlotte Perriand (b. 1903)

A partner of Le Corbusier and Pierre Jeanneret in the design of furniture in the late 1920s, Charlotte Perriand, the French architect, is an innovative architect whose prewar experience with Jean Prouvé, an extended stay in Japan, and her postwar partnership with Paul Nelson and Fernand Léger have helped establish her as a leading architect.

430. *Meribel.* Chair. Ashwood. 17¾ x 14⅞ x 32″. Sentou

431. *Courchevel.* Chair. Ashwood. 16⅜ x 16⅜ x 29¼″. Sentou

432. *Chamrousse.* Armchair. Ashwood. 22⅝ x 24⅛ x 30½″. Sentou

433. Three-leg low stool. Ashwood. Sentou

434. *Orcieres.* Four-leg stool. Ashwood. 14 x 14 x 17½″. Sentou

Gaetano Pesce (b. 1939)

Gaetano Pesce is an Italian architect whose furniture and objects continually challenge the conformism of "good design." Pesce believes in the as-yet-unexplored application of today's technology and the possibilities that will emerge from it. For him the future will not be a replica of the past, a philosophy reflected in his designs.

435. *Serie "Luigi"* or *"Mi Amate Voi?"* Object stand. Frame in lacquered nonhomogeneous black with shelves in plywood color or decorated in different ways on both sides with natural edges. 32⅗ x 32¾ x 74⅛″. G. B. Bernini

436a–b. *Serie "Luigi"* or *"Mi Amate Voi?"* Folding table. Frame in maple, lacquered in nonhomogeneous orange; top comprises four circular parts in plywood, lacquered black or white or in white opaque laminate on the surfaces with natural edges. Diameter 50″; height 28½″. G.B. Bernini

437. *Serie "Luigi"* or *"Mi Amate Voi?"* Wall object stand. Frame in maple, lacquered in nonhomogeneous black; fixed to the wall by orange ball placed at top of each element; shelves of four different dimensions in plywood colored or decorated in different ways on both surfaces with natural edges; adjustable shelves fixed in horizontal or vertical positions. Wall stand height 81⅞″; shelves available in variety of widths, depths, and heights. G.B. Bernini

438. *Serie "Luigi"* or *"Mi Amate Voi?"* Screen with adjustable shelves. Base in natural or lacquered lead; frame in maple, lacquered in nonhomogeneous orange, blue, or green; shelves in two different shapes and several dimensions made out of plywood and colored white, yellow, red, or green exclusively on both surfaces with natural edges in maple. 17½–23¾ x 17½–47¼ x 70¼″. G. B. Bernini

439a–b. *Serie Sit-Down.* Armchair and sofa. 1976. Foam polyurethane structure; padding injected into a Dacron tufting cover; mutli-plywood base; upholstery in special fabric or from selected Cassina collection. Armchair 44½ x 34⅜ x 28½″; sofa 66⅜ x 34⅜ x 28½″. Ottoman also available. Cassina

440. *Sansone.* Table. 1980. Polychrome table in polyester resin, molded by casting; available in three color combinations: white/green/red, blue/red/yellow, or blue/white/red. Custom ordered to size. Cassina

441a–c. *Dalila Uno, Due, Tre.* Chairs. 1980. Molded hard polyurethane; gray, black, or brick red epoxy finish. *Uno* 19⅛ x 21½ x 34¾″; *Due* 20⅝ x 23¾ x 29¼″; *Tre* 27⅝ x 24⅞ x 32⅜″. Cassina

442. *Sunset in New York.* Three-seat sofa. 1980. Multi-plywood frame and foam polyurethane and Dacron padding; upholstery in special fabric. 87¾ x 40⅞ x 46⅞″. Cassina

Warren Platner (b. 1919)

A long-time associate of Eero Saarinen, the American architect Warren Platner began his own architectural and interior design practice in Connecticut in 1968 and for several years collaborated with the Knoll Design Development Group.

443. Lounge chair. Steel rod base electrically welded with bright nickel finish; seat and back foam cushion over molded fiberglass shell. 36½ x 25½ x 30½″. Knoll International

444. Ottoman. Steel rod base electrically welded with bright nickel finish; seat foam cushion over molded fiberglass shell. Diameter 24½″; height 15″. Knoll International

445. Armchair. Steel rod base electrically welded with bright nickel finish; seat molded rubber suspension unit. 26½ x 22 x 29″. Knoll International

446. Easy chair. Steel rod base electrically welded with bright nickel finish; seat and back foam cushion over molded fiberglass shell. 40¾ x 36½ x 39″. Knoll International

Gio Ponti (1897–1979)

Painter, industrial designer, architect, and founding editor of the architecture and design magazine Domus, *Gio Ponti was a member of the Rational Architecture Group and a pioneer of the modern movement in Italy. His building for the Faculty of Mathematics in Rome and his Montecatini headquarters and Pirelli Building in Milan established Ponti as one of Italy's most famous architects.*

447. *Lama.* Door handle. Satin brass. Length 4⅝″. Window handle also available. Olivari

448. Appliqué light fixture. Lacquered metal; 60-watt bulb. Width 6½″; height 17½″. Candle

449. Appliqué light fixtures. Brass; six, ten, fourteen, or eighteen 25-watt bulbs. Left to right: Width 5⅛″, height 19⅛″; width 8⅞″, height 19⅛″; width 12⅞″, height 19⅛″; width 16¾″, height 19⅛″. Candle

450. *Superlegerra.* Chair. 1957. Ashtree frame, natural or black or white lacquered; special caning. 16 x 18⅜ x 32⅜″. Cassina

Anna Praun

Anna Praun practices architecture in Austria, where she designs family houses, boats, interiors, and furniture.

451. Nesting tables. Massive beech; transparent varnish. Largest to smallest: 21½ x 18⅞ x 20⅞″; 20 x 17⅜ x 19⅞″; 17½ x 15⅞ x 18⅞″. Holzwerkstätten

404

405

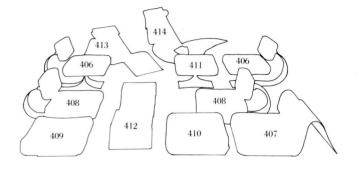

415

416

417

418

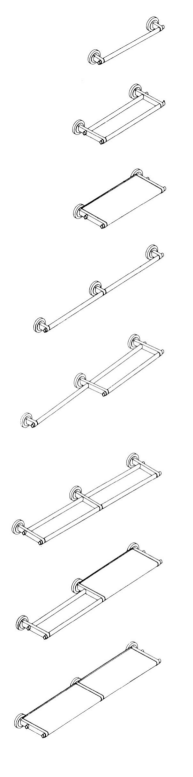

419

420 a

420 b

420 c

421

422

422

423

424

425

426

427

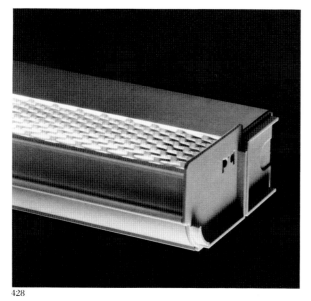

428

429

430

431

432

433

434

435

436a

436b

437

438

439a

439 b

440

441a

441b

441c

442

443

444

445

446

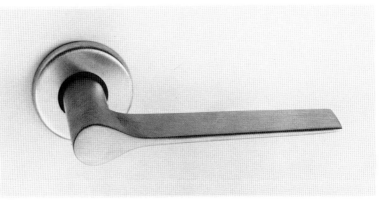

447

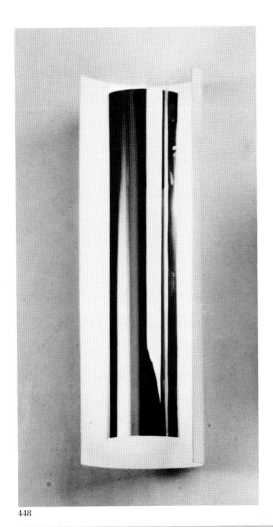

448

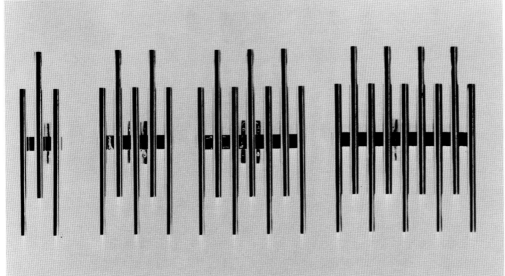

449

451

RS

Sybold van Ravesteyn

Gerrit Rietveld

Aldo Rossi and Luca Meda

Eero Saarinen

Carlo Scarpa

Rainer Schell

Alvaro Siza

Paolo Soleri

Johannes Spalt

Mart Stam

SUPERSTUDIO

Sybold van Ravesteyn (b. 1889)

As a member of the De Stijl group, van Ravesteyn applied the Cubist experience to his own designs. His handling of contrasting vertical and horizontal plans and his mastering of basic colors were among the best of the times.

452. Table lamps. Nickel-plated tubing and lacquered wood. Ecart International
453. Chair. 1925. Lacquered wood. Ecart International/ Pallucco

Gerrit Rietveld (1888–1964)

In 1918 the Dutch architect and cabinetmaker Gerrit Rietveld designed his famous Red and Blue Chair. It was a prophetic manifesto of modern architecture, its supporting framework and brightly colored planes foretelling the simplistic rationalities of the movement.

After his introduction to Theo van Doesburg and to other members of the De Stijl group, Rietveld pursued his quest for an almost total geometric abstraction and designed the Schröder House in Utrecht, a crystallization of the De Stijl aesthetic.

In the 1950s Rietveld's projects included the Amsterdam Institute for the Applied Arts and the Van Slobbe House, both masterpieces of contemporary northern European architecture.

454. *Red and Blue Chair.* Lounge chair. 1918. Beechwood frame, black and yellow aniline finish; seat in blue lacquer finish, back in red lacquer finish. 25⅞ x 32¼ x 34⅜". Cassina
455. *Schroeder 1.* Low table. Lacquered wood. 19½ x 20⅛ x 23⅝". Cassina
456. *Zig-Zag.* Side chair. 1934. Unfinished or finished elm. 14⅜ x 16¾ x 28⅞". Cassina
457. *Crate 4.* Table. 1934. Solid unfinished beechwood frame and top. 68¼ x 29⅝ x 27¾". Cassina
458. *Crate 7.* Writing desk. 1934. Solid unfinished beechwood. 46⅞ x 23⅜ x 15¼". Cassina
459. *Crate 5.* Armchair. 1934. Solid unfinished beechwood. 21½ x 23 x 15¼". Cassina
460. *Crate 3.* Bookshelves. 1934. Solid unfinished beechwood. Cassina
461. *Crate 2.* Low table. 1934. Solid unfinished beechwood. 23⅜ x 23⅜ x 17⅛". Cassina
462. *Crate 1.* Lounge chair. 1934. Solid unfinished beechwood; cushion optional. 21⅞ x 27⅜ x 24⅛". Cassina
463. *Crate 6.* Stool. 1934. Solid unfinished beechwood. Cassina

Aldo Rossi (b. 1931)
Luca Meda

One of the most prominent spokesmen for European Post-Modern rationalism is the Italian architect Aldo Rossi, who considers its philosophy the perpetuation of eighteenth-century enlightenment. His theories on the nature of cities and his historical investigations have brought him to the conclusion that "the reductible specificity of architecture [has] resided in the capacity to produce typical forms."

464a–b. *Capitolo.* Two- or three-seat sofa and armchair. Metal frame overlaid with resilient polyurethane; legs in turned wood; white cotton undercover; seat and back cushions in quilted material; leather upholstery and marble legs optional. Armchair 40⅞ x 35⅛ x 29¼"; two-seat sofa 61¼ x 35⅛ x 29¼"; three-seat sofa 82¼ x 35⅛ x 29¼". Molteni

465. *Cabina Armadio.* Cupboard. Lacquered wood. 63½ x 33⅛ x 107¼". Molteni

Eero Saarinen (1910–1961)

The son of the famous Finnish architect Eliel Saarinen, Eero Saarinen completed his studies at Yale and entered into partnership with his father, who was then teaching at the Cranbrook Academy of Art in Michigan. Eero's winning of the Jefferson Memorial Competition in St. Louis in 1949 established his own identity as an architect and placed him firmly in the field.

In the early 1950s Saarinen designed the General Motors Technical Center in Warren, Michigan, the first in a long series of brilliant projects. Each commission became a new challenge for him, which he resolved each time with new functional solutions and formal expressions. His buildings include the Kresge Auditorium and Chapel at the Massachusetts Institute of Technology in Cambridge; two buildings for IBM; the John Deere headquarters in Moline, Illinois; the Yale University Hockey Rink; and the TWA Terminal at Kennedy Airport.

In 1940 Saarinen won the "Organic Design in Home Furnishing" competition for his and Charles Eames's chair design. He was soon commissioned to

design furniture for the then young, innovative firm Knoll. Today his chairs, armchairs, and tables are best-selling items as well as timeless classics.

466. Open back chair. Leg base in tubular steel with polished chrome finish; frame in reinforced plastic shell with contour plywood seat form; upholstery covered with fabric. 22¼ x 20¼ x 32″. Knoll International
467. Easy chair and ottoman. 1948. Steel rod base with polished chrome finish; chair upholstery, foam over molded plastic shell; ottoman upholstery, foam cushion over molded plywood platform loose cushions; covered with fabric. Chair 40 x 34 x 35½″; ottoman 25½ x 20 x 16″. Knoll International
468. Tables. 1956. Cast metal base with fused finish; top in oak or walnut veneer, white plastic laminate, or Italian marble. Round coffee table diameter 36″, height 15″; round side table diameter 16″, height 20½″; round dining table diameter 42″, height 28½″; oval dining table 78 x 48 x 28½″. Knoll International
469. Side chair and armchairs. 1956. Cast aluminum base, white fused finish; molded plastic shell with white lacquer finish; wool cushions and upholstery. Armchair with cushion 26 x 23½ x 32″; upholstered armchair 26 x 23½ x 32¾″; side chair 19½ x 22 x 32½″. Knoll International
470. Stool. 1956. Cast aluminum base, white fused finish; molded plastic shell with white lacquer finish; cushion covered with fabric. Diameter 15″; height 16″. Knoll International

Carlo Scarpa (1906–1978)

Strongly influenced by the architecture of Frank Lloyd Wright, the Venetian architect Carlo Scarpa learned from this modern master how to handle space, volume, light, and how to coordinate different materials. Scarpa's skills and talents revolutionized the art of museum display and were reflected in his pavilions at the Venice Biennale and in his extensions and fittings for museums throughout Italy.

471. Book case. 1935. Wood and metal. 81½ x 17⅞ x 92⅞–116¼″. G.B. Bernini
472. *Zibaldone*. Book case. Wood and glass. G.B. Bernini
473. Bastiano lounge chair. 1968. Oak, walnut, Honduras mahogany, or rosewood frame; separate cushions of foam over rubber and steel suspension covered with fabric, leather, or vinyl. 36 x 32 x 27″. Settee and sofa also available. Knoll International.

474a. *Franzo Serie*. Table (rectangular or square). 1934. Wood. 77¼ x 55¾ x 27⅞″. G.B. Bernini
474b. *Franzo Serie*. Chair. 1934. Wooden frame; leather seat/back. 19½ x 19½ x 40⅛″. G.B. Bernini

475. *Franzo Serie*. Sideboard. 1934. Wood. 106½ x 23 x 39¾″. G.B. Bernini
476. Nibay extension table. 1968. Natural or ebonized oak, walnut, or rosewood. 57 x 39 x 28″; extended 57 x 78 x 27½″. Knoll International
477. *Franzo Serie*. Sideboard. 1934. Wood. 38¼ x 17½ x 72⅞″. G.B. Bernini
478. *Franzo Serie*. Sideboard. 1934. Wood. 60⅝ x 17½ x 35⅛″. G.B. Bernini
479. *Franzo Serie*. Square table. 1934. Wood. 60 x 60 x 27⅞″. G.B. Bernini
480. *Franzo Serie*. Chair. 1934. Wood. 17⅛ x 17⅛ x 35½″. G.B. Bernini
481. Tray. Silver 800. Rossi & Arcandi
482. Tray. Silver 800. Rossi & Arcandi
483. Cutlery. Gold or silver 800. Rossi & Arcandi
484. Pitcher. Silver 800. Rossi & Arcandi
485. Flower vase. Glass. Venini
486. Fruit tray. Silver 800. Rossi & Arcandi

Rainer Schell (b. 1917)

Rainer Schell has been a practicing architect in West Germany since 1950 with an interest in modular-system furniture.

487. *Series 64*. Modular furniture system. Chairs, armchairs, tables, shelves, and cupboards; ash or beechwood with nongloss or color-stained surface; white plastic doors and table tops; upholstery covered with canvas. Dimensions vary according to style. Schlapp-Möbel

Alvaro Siza (b. 1933)

Alvaro Siza—trained and practicing in Porto, Portugal—has integrated the gains of modernism and the controversial theories of Post-Modernism into his own original architecture. Siza's projects are rooted in the vernacular building tradition of Porto and reflect his attempt to answer, architecturally, the social, economic, and political problems of Portugal. His commitment to social housing demonstrates this dimension of his work, a commitment that has also influenced his designs for elegant homes and local banks.

488. *Flamingo.* Floor lamp. Dismountable frame in chromium-plated tubing and rod; adjustable stainless steel wings for controlling light. 35⅞–29⅝ x 46⅞ x 46⅞–33⅛″. B.D. Ediciones

Paolo Soleri (b. 1919)

After his training at the Turin Polytechnic, the Italian-born Paolo Soleri took up an apprenticeship with Frank Lloyd Wright in Arizona and later settled there. In the early 1950s he returned to Italy and built a ceramics factory at Vietri sul Mare near Salerno.

Back in Arizona, Soleri experimented with ecological building techniques and designed a utopian urban alternative to contemporary cities called Arcosanti, a project now under construction.

In addition to his architectural activities, Soleri designs and produces handmade ceramic or bronze windbells, which provide financial income for the continued realization of his utopian city.

489. Ceramic windbells. Handcrafted ceramic. Cosanti Originals, Inc.
490. Ceramic bell assemblies. Handcrafted ceramic. Cosanti Originals, Inc.
491. Bronze windbells. Styrofoam casting; finishes in burnished bronze, bronze patina, or combination of bronze and aluminum. Cosanti Originals, Inc.
492. Bell trees. Cosanti Originals, Inc.

Johannes Spalt (b. 1920)

Johannes Spalt is director of the Vienna School of Applied Arts, a practicing architect, and a professor of architecture in various Austrian academies.

493. *Table 1.* Dining-room table. Top in blue, red, or green linoleum framed with massive pine; legs in pine with transparent varnish. 58½ x 29¼ x 28¼″. Holzwerkstätten
494. *Table 2.* Square table. Top in blue, red, or green linoleum framed with massive pine; legs in pine with transparent varnish. 19½ x 19½ x 19½″. Holzwerkstätten
495. *Table 3.* Low table. Top in blue, red, or green linoleum framed with massive pine; legs in pine. 19½ x 19½ x 12⅝″. Holzwerkstätten

Mart Stam (b. 1899)

Mart Stam was a member, with Hannes Mèyer and El Lissitzky, of the left-wing avant garde, a guest lecturer at the Bauhaus, and one of the coauthors of the famous concluding declaration of the first CIAM (Congrès Internationaux d'Architecture Moderne).

In the early 1930s Stam went as a specialist to the U.S.S.R., but was later dismissed. His faith in the socialist credo was reflected, however, in his designs for numerous Constructivist and functionalist urban planning and architectural projects, some of which were actually built.

496. Cantilevered armchair. 1925. Bent and chrome-plated steel tubes; seat and back covered with natural cowhide. 22⅝ x 24⅞ x 33⅛″. Thonet (West Germany)
497. Cantilevered chair. Bent and chrome-plated steel tubes; seat and back covered with natural cowhide. 19½ x 22¼ x 33⅛″. Thonet (West Germany)
498. Cantilevered armchair. Bent and chrome-plated steel tubes; seat and back caned. 23 x 22¼ x 31¼″. Thonet (West Germany)
499. Cantilevered chair. Bent and chrome-plated steel tubes; seat and back caned. 17½ x 22¼ x 31¼″. Thonet (West Germany)
500. Cantilevered armchair. Bent and chrome-plated steel tubes; seat and back upholstered. 23 x 22¼ x 31¼″. Thonet (West Germany)
501. Cantilevered chair. Bent and chrome-plated steel tubes; seat and back upholstered. 17½ x 22¼ x 31¼″. Thonet (West Germany)
502. Armchair. 1926. Polished stainless steel frame; oak veneer-molded plywood for seat and back; solid oak armrests. 22½ x 22 x 33″. Thonet (U.S.)
503. Side chair. 1926. Polished stainless steel; oak veneer-molded plywood for seat and back. 16⅝ x 20⅝ x 30⅞″. Thonet (U.S.)

SUPERSTUDIO

SUPERSTUDIO is a group of Italian designers based in Florence, which was created in 1966. Its members are interested in architectural theory and system design.

504a–d. *Quaderna.* Table, desk, bench, and console. Stratified plywood construction covered with white plastic laminate; silkscreen printed with black squares. Table 43¼ x 43¼ x 28″; desk 70¼ x 31½ x 28″; bench 16⅜ x 58½ x 15¼″; console 70¼ x 16⅜ x 32¾″. Zanotta

452

453

454

455

456

457

458

459

463

460 461 462

464 a 464 b

465

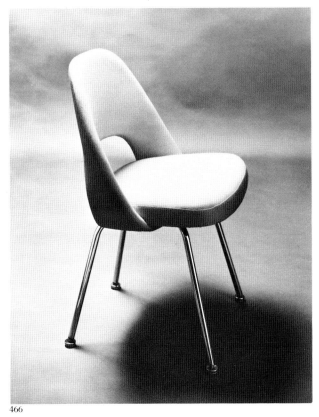

466

467

468 469 470

471

472

473

474a 474b

475

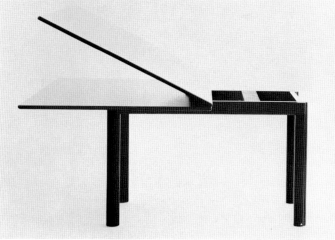

476

477

480

478

479

481

482

483

484

485

486

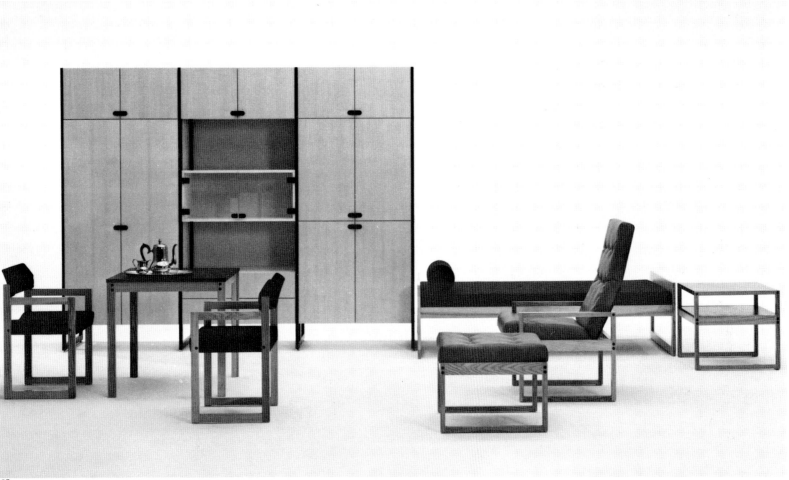

487

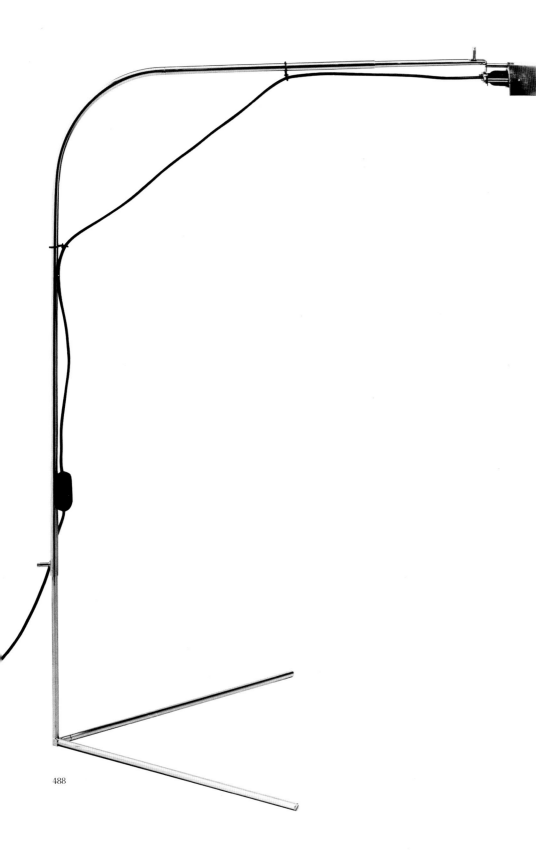

488

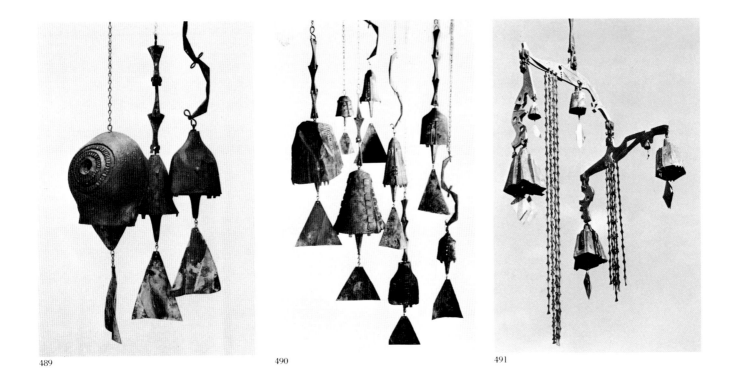

489

490

491

492

493

494

495

496

497

498

499

500

501

502

503

504a

504b

504c

504d

Vladimir Tatlin

Giuseppe Terragni

Otto Wagner

Stephan Wewerka

Carl Witzmann

Vladimir Tatlin (1885–1953)

Vladimir Tatlin was a Russian Constructivist whose monument to the Third International was never constructed but won international attention. His works were later overshadowed by the official Stalinist "realism" and rediscovered in the mid-1960s.

505. Armchair. 1927. Frame in chrome tubing; cushion covered with black leather. Nikol Internazionale

Giuseppe Terragni (1904–1942)

The Italian architect Giuseppe Terragni was among the few who, under the fascist regime, fought for a new approach to architecture. Along with Gio Ponti he formed the Movement for Rational Architecture and in 1938 designed the Como Casa del Popolo, an architectural achievement.

506. *Novocomun*. Side table. 1929. Palm tree root veneer or black lacquered. Diameter 35⅛; height 23″. B.D. Ediciones
507. *Monza*. Armchair. 1930. Frame in bentwood tinted black; back and seat cushions in polyurethane covered with fabric. 26⅞ x 37½ x 23⅜″. B.D. Ediciones
508. *Lariana*. Chair. 1936. Frame in stainless steel chrome tubing; seat and back in pressed beech plywood. 16⅜ x 21⅞ x 30⅞″. Zanotta
509. *Benita*. Armchair. Structure in chromium-plated steel, seat, back, and armrests upholstered. 24⅛ x 27¼ x 29¼″. Zanotta
510. *Follia*. Chair. Solid wood, black lacquered; back support, stainless steel. 19½ x 19½ x 31¼″. Zanotta

Otto Wagner (1841–1918)

Founder of the modern movement in Austria, the architect Otto Wagner inaugurated his professorship at the Vienna Academy in 1895 by declaring war against nineteenth-century stylistic revivals: "We do not walk around in the costumes of Louis XIV," he announced. Wagner's aim was to find a new response to "modern life," a subject later developed by the Viennese architect Adolf Loos.

Wagner applied his concepts to housing developments in Vienna and to stations for the city's railway system, among the latter, the Karlsplatz station. He also supported the Secession movement,

and his design for the Majolika house in 1898 expressed his commitment to this new mood. Perhaps his best-known buildings were the Vienna Postal Savings Bank and his church for the Am Steinhof asylum outside Vienna.

511. Armchair. 1900-1906. Curved wood with or without upholstery; bottom protection in polished brass. Thonet (West Germany)
512. *Wiener Postparkasse Serie*. Stool. 1904. Steam-bent American elm leg and seat frame; molded plywood seat. 16¼ x 16¼ x 18½″. Thonet (U.S.)
513. *Tramway*. Ceiling lamp. Diameter 11¾″; height 9⅜″. Woka
514. *Wiener Postparkasse Serie*. Table (round or oval). 1900. Beech tree tinted; bottom protection in polished brass. Thonet (West Germany)

Stephan Wewerka (b. 1928)

Stephan Wewerka practices in West Germany.

515. Three-leg chair. Solid ashwood, black or white lacquered; upholstery covered with special fabric. Tecta
516. Office table. Ashwood veneer, white or black lacquered. Tecta
517. Chair. Ashwood tinted black; seat and back caned. Tecta
518. Conference table. Ashwood veneer, with Carrare marble and glass. Tecta
519. Low table. Plexiglas. Tecta
520. Cupboard. Ashwood veneer, black tinted. Tecta
521. Sofa with cushions. Tecta
522. High-back sofa with cushions. Tecta
523. Armchair. Tecta
524. Steel object. Steel. Tecta

Carl Witzmann (1883–1952)

Carl Witzmann studied under Josef Hoffmann before teaching interior and furniture design in Vienna. In 1923 he became director of the Department of Interior and Furniture Design, a position he held until 1949.

525. *Apollo*. Ceiling lamp. Diameter 10⅛″; height 3½″. Woka
526. *Apollo*. Globe appliqué lamp. 7⅛ x 8⅞ x 5½″. Woka
527. *Apollo*. Appliqué lamp. Diameter 5½″; height 11¾″. Woka

505

267

506

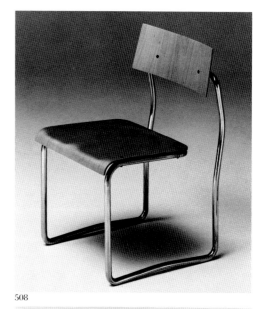

508

509

507

510

511

513

512

514

515 516

517 518

519

520

521

522

523

524

525

526

527

Addendum

Gunnar Asplund (1885–1940)

Chief-architect of the influential 1930 Stockholm Exhibition, Asplund is known for his designs of Scandinavian classicism. His Stockholm City Library (1924–27) and Crematorium, Stockholm South Cemetery (1935–40), granted him international fame. Asplund also designed furniture for the Stockholm City Hall and for the Nordisk Kompaniet; these neoclassical pieces are now being reissued.

528. *Göteborg 1*. Side chair. 1934–37. Walnut or ash-wood frame with natural or stained walnut finish; leather upholstery. 15¾ x 20½ x 31½". Cassina

529. *Göteborg 2*. Armchair. 1934–37. Walnut frame with natural finish; self-supporting leather seat and back. 29⅞ x 30⅓ x 34½". Cassina

530. *Senna*. Lounge chair. 1925. Walnut frame with natural finish; leather upholstery with silk-screen design printed after original Asplund drawing process. 36¼ x 42 x 44⅞". Cassina

Atelier Zo
Kasumasa Sakamoto, Kinya Maruyama

Atelier Zo is an informal group of Japanese architects who, through their romantic, apparently free-form building designs, maintain a rational but unorthodox interpretation of Japanese architectural traditions.

531. *Hanako*. Chair. Limetree plywood. 24⅞ x 24⅜ x 26⅓". Hoekan

532. *Taro*. High-back chair. Limetree plywood. 24⅞ x 24⅞ x 59⅞". Hoekan

Helmut Bätzner (b. 1925)

German architect Bätzner's design for an all-plastic chair for the new Karlsruhe Theater (1964) was considered a technological feat as well as a world premiere.

533. Triangular stool. 1964. Polyester resin reinforced with fiberglass. Top, each side 15¾"; height 14⅞. Bermude; Habit

534. Chair. 1964. Polyester resin reinforced with fiberglass. 20⅞ x 20⅞ x 29½". Bermude; Habit

Werner Blaser (b. 1924)

Professor of architecture at the University of Basel, Blaser is a practicing architect and one of the best exponents of modern or vernacular architecture. His books and exhibitions on the subjects of Japanese temples and teahouses, Mies van der Rohe, and Eastern structural architecture are internationally known.

535. *Blaser*. Armchair. 1958. Tubular steel frame with stitched belting-leather seat, back, and armrests. 21 x 23½ x 33½". Larsen Furniture

536. *Blaser*. Side chair. 1958. Tubular steel frame with stitched belting-leather seat and back. 20½ x 23½ x 33½". Larsen Furniture

537. *Blaser*. Lounge armchair. 1958. Tubular steel frame with stitched belting-leather seat, back, and armrests. 30 x 27½ x 31¼". Larsen Furniture

Mario Botta (b. 1943)

One of the best representatives of the Swiss-Italian Tendenza, a rationalist movement that appeared in the late 1950s, Botta became internationally famous through publications of small, well-designed private houses built in his native Tessin. In 1986 Botta received the Chicago Architectural Award.

538. *Melanos*. Table lamp. Extendable arm in black plastic. 33⅞ x 33½". Artemide

539. *Prima*. Chair. Galvanized steel epoxy-painted frame in metallized silver and dull black; perforated steel seat enamelled in metal silver and dull black; back with two rotating cylindrical elements in soft expanded black polyurethane. 18⅞ x 22⅞ x 28⅜". Alias

540. *Seconda*. Chair with armrests. Galvanized steel epoxy-painted frame in metallized silver and dull black; perforated steel seat enamelled in metal silver and dull black; back with two rotating cylindrical elements in soft expanded black polyurethane. 20½ x 22⅞ x 28⅜". Alias

541. *Sesta*. Sofa. Perforated and stretched steel frame painted with black epoxy powder; seat and cushion in high-density expanded polyurethane. 39⅜ x 39⅜ x 37⅜". Alias

Pierre Chareau (1883–1950)

Chareau is famous in the architectural world for his celebrated masterpiece, the Maison de Verre in Paris (1928–31), designed for Dr. Jean Dalsace in collaboration with Bernard Bijvoet, and for his design for artist Robert Motherwell's house in East Hampton, New York (1940; now demolished). Chareau was known in the 1930s as an elegant and imaginative furniture and interior designer using rare materials in sophisticated ways.

542. Trunk. 1927. Stained walnut burl exterior encircled with a thick sheet of folded patined steel; interior in sycamore. 28 x 18 x 51″. Ecart International

543. *Fan Table.* Side table. 1920. Waxed, patined wrought iron; the two fan-shaped pieces rotate. Diameter 23″; height 23½″. Ecart International

544. *"T".* Stool. 1928. Waxed, patined wrought iron with varnished concave seat of rosewood or black-stained mahogany. 19¼ x 16 x 19″. Ecart International

Norman Foster (b. 1935)

Although opposed to those who believe High-Tech to be the sole architectural expression of advanced technologies, Foster uses High-Tech materials and techniques to design elegant forms and develop refined spaces. His ideals are best achieved in his Sainsbury Centre for Visual Arts at the University of East Anglia (1978) and the headquarters of the HongKong and Shanghai Banking Corporation in Hong Kong (1986), two masterpieces constructed of steel and glass.

545. *Nomos.* Desk. Chromed steel frame with clear glass rectangular or round top. Dimensions vary according to style. Tecno

Josef Frank (1885–1985)

Viennese by birth, in training, and in concepts, Frank moved in 1934 to Sweden, where, through a long collaboration with Svenskt Tenn, he developed what was later called "The Swedish Grace," a refined, modern bourgeois furniture and interior design which, respecting Modern Movement principles, responded to more popular tastes. His teaching at the New School for Social Research in New York (1941–46) was quietly but firmly opposed to the then prevailing Bauhaus furniture dogmas. In fact,

Frank considered chairs as complements to human bodies rather than as mere combinations of geometric forms, which he declared totalitarian.

546. *Nationalmuseiskap.* Cupboard. Walnut and root of vanonna; brass handles. 35⅜ x 17¾ x 47¼″. Svenskt Tenn

547. Armchair. Mahogany; seat upholstered with green or red leather. 21¼ x 22⅞ x 41⅓″. Svenskt Tenn

548. Cupboard. Cherrywood and glass. 35⅜ x 11⅞ x 32¼″. Svenskt Tenn

549. *"U.S. Tree."* Decorative fabric. Linen. Width 51³⁄₁₆″. Svenskt Tenn

550. *"Vegetable Tree."* Decorative fabric. Linen. Width 51³⁄₁₆″. Svenskt Tenn

Ignazio Gardella (b. 1905)

As architect, Gardella is famed for the purist, elegant, and somewhat poetic qualities of his numerous buildings and for his refusal to commit to current ideologies, trends, or polemics. He first became known with his design for a medical center (1938) for the city of Alessandria, where most of his work stands. Among his other achievements are a magnificent house on the Venice Grand Canal and the Olivetti Research Center in Ivrea (1959). Gardella's furniture designs reflect the sober clarity of his production.

551. *Idillio.* Table. Polished polyester lacquered in black, ice white, or bordeaux base composed of two 1″-thick rounded massive pieces of wood linked with brass elements; Carrara marble or wooden top. Width 51³⁄₁₆–74⅞″; depth 51³⁄₁₆″; height 29⅛″. Misura Emme

552. *Ditirambo.* Table. 1949. Metallic base varnished with epoxy and finished in brass tone; lacquered wooden top. Widths 51¼″ and 98¾″; depth 47¼″; height 28¾″. Misura Emme

553. *Partenio.* Table. Wooden base lacquered with polyester; marble extendable top. Widths 51³⁄₁₆″ and 74⅞″; depth 51¾″; height 29⅛″. Misura Emme

554. *Madia Epillio.* Modular cupboard. Lacquered wooden structure with Carrara marble top; doors and drawers in lacquered polyester; available in black, white, ice, or bordeaux. Width of modules 18½″ and 20⁷⁄₁₆″; depth 17¾″; height 47¼″. Misura Emme

555. *Pindaro.* Bed and table. Polyester lacquered wood; dark or light gray, ice, bordeaux, or black. 69⅓ x 77½ x 33⅛″. Misura Emme

Steven Holl (b. 1947)

Besides maintaining an active professional practice as designer of several highly acclaimed private homes, Holl teaches at Columbia University, Pratt Institute, the University of Pennsylvania, and Parsons School of Design. He has also received grants from the New York State Council on the Arts, the Graham Foundation, and the National Endowment for the Arts for his original research on contemporary architecture.

556. *K Desk.* Desk. Wooden structure with natural ash or black finish; leather top; footcaps in brass with waxen green patina finish. 46 x 28⅞ x 41⅓". i4 Mariani

557. *K Sofa.* Love seat or three-seat sofa. Black matte wooden frame; upholstered in exclusive fabric or leather. Love seat 63⅓ x 21⅓ x 29⅞"; three-seat sofa 96¹⁄₁₆ x 21⅓ x 29⅞". i4 Mariani

Arata Isozaki (b. 1931)

Isozaki, chief-architect of Expo '70 in Osaka, and one of Japan's leading talents, demonstrates strong affinities for American Post-Modernism, as seen in his designs for The Museum of Contemporary Art in Los Angeles (1986) and the Palladium nightclub in New York City (1985).

558. Wristwatch. Cleto Munari

559. *Monroe.* Oval, round, or triangular table. Wooden base and veneer top with natural or black finish. Oval table 95¼ x 60¼ x 28"; round table, diameter 82", height 28"; triangular table, each side of top 70¼", height 28". SunarHauserman

560. *Monroe.* Chair. Wooden frame with natural or black finish; seat upholstered in leather. 20½ x 21 x 55". SunarHauserman

Bruno Paul (1874–1968)

A founding member, in 1907, of the Deutscher Werkbund and director of the School of the Museum of Arts and Crafts Berlin, Paul took, in 1924, the direction of the United Schools for Free and Applied Arts (now called College of Arts), from which he resigned in 1932 for political reasons. His most important constructions are the Völkerkundemuseum and the Kathreiner building (1929–30), Berlin's first skyscraper.

561. *West End.* Table. 1911. Base of five channeled pillars; wooden top with inlaid veneer of walnut with black grain and polyester finish. 49¼ x 49¼ x 29⅛". Vereinigte Werkstätten

562. *Washington.* Table. 1908. Black granite base; frame and extendable wooden top with gloss lacquer finish in dark gray. 55⅛ x 39⅜ x 28⅜". Vereinigte Werkstätten

Renzo Piano (b. 1937)

Famous for his original and provocative Centre Pompidou in Paris (1971–77; in partnership with Richard Rogers), Piano is now considered one of the best Italian architects, practicing in Genoa, Paris, and Houston, Texas.

563. *Teso.* High and low tables. Base made of two massive joint blocks of crystal; stratified finished crystal top. Dimensions vary according to style. Fontana Arte

Paolo Portoghesi (b. 1931)

Publisher of the Italian magazines Controspazio *and* Eupalino *and of numerous books on ancient and contemporary architecture, Portoghesi is known for his Islamic Centre and Mosque in Rome (1976) and buildings in Sudan and the Middle East. He has been, since 1983, chairman of the Venice Biennale.*

564. Teapot from six-piece coffee and tea service. Silver 925/1000; with decorative band engraved and enamelled in black and white; ebony handle. Alessi

565. *Gruppo Liuto.* Two-seat sofa. Iron frame; polyurethane and dracon upholstery; base and decoration in cherrywood, stained walnut, or white or lacquered beech. 63⅜ x 31½ x 27⅞". Poltronova

566. *Gruppo Liuto.* Low square, round, or oval table. Frame in cherrywood; stained walnut, or white or green lacquered beech; clear glass top. Dimensions vary according to style. Poltronova

Jean Prouvé (1901–1984)

Specializing in light-metal construction and totally industrialized buildings, Prouvé was one of the foremost modern French architect-engineers. The elegant ingenuity of his designs led him to collaborate with Le Corbusier and Robert Mallet-Stevens

and, later, to investigate comprehensively and develop numerous projects constructed of metal: prefabricated homes and schools, low-cost housing and cultural facilities, curtain-wall façades, and the gracious lakeshore buvette of Evian (1957). His furniture is also constructed of metal but reflects more strongly his personal wit.

567.   Adjustable lounge chair. 1930. Handmade nickel-plated sheet-metal frame; black-coated sheet-metal seat upholstered in cavalry cloth or leather; head-roll. 24⅞ x 49¼ x 38⅞". Tecta Möbel

568.   High-back chair. 1924. Handmade nickel-plated sheet-metal frame; back and seat cushions covered with black cavalry cloth. 17¾ x 20 x 40½". Tecta Möbel

569.   Armchair. 1927. Epoxy-lacquered steel frame; seat in raw cotton cloth. 28⅜ x 34⅔ x 33⅓". Bermude

570.   Chair. 1923–25. Epoxy-lacquered steel frame; seat and back in dull varnished beech plywood. 15¾ x 15¾ x 31½". Bermude

571.   Table. 1950. Epoxy-lacquered steel frame; thick glass top. 86⅝ x 47¼ x 28⅓". Bermude

572.   Round table. 1935. Epoxy-lacquered steel frame; laminated plastic, solid beech, or glass top; legs in solid beech. Diameter 47"; height 28⅓". Bermude

Richard Riemerschmid (1868–1957)

Among Riemerschmid's first designs as architect were those for his own house and furniture, an art-lover room for the 1900 Paris Exposition, and a director's room for the 1904 St. Louis Exposition—all extremely well considered. He designed also, in 1898, furniture for the Munich Vereinigte Werkstätten and, in 1904, mass-produced pieces. Co-founder of the Deutscher Werkbund, he later directed the Munich School of Applied Arts (1912–24) and the Industrial School of Cologne (1926–31).

573.   Armchair. Solid European beech frame; assorted finishes; upholstered in fabric and leathers; French natural brass nail trim. 23¼ x 23¼ x 31". Larsen Furniture

574.   Music-room chair. Solid European beech frame; assorted finishes; upholstered in fabric and leathers; French natural brass nail trim. 19½ x 23¾ x 31¼". Larsen Furniture

Eliel Saarinen (1873–1950)

Trained simultaneously as painter and architect, Saarinen practiced first in Finland, where he built the Helsinki Railway Station (1904–16) in a romantic, nationalistic interpretation of classicism. After receiving second prize with a submission in the 1922 Chicago Tribune competition, he moved to America in 1923 and became visiting professor at the University of Michigan. With the help of George Booth, owner of the Detroit News, *Saarinen developed in 1925 the Cranbrook Educational Community, which later became the Cranbrook Academy of Art. His best-known American works are the Cranbrook School (1925) and Christ Church Cranbrook in Minneapolis (1925–26).*

575.   *Blue Suite.* Armchair. 1929. Solid birch frame gray-blue lacquered with gold leaf; foam-padded seat upholstered with fabric designed by Irma Kukkasjärvi. 25 x 19⅞ x 29⅞". Adelta Oy

576.   *Saarinen House Dining Chair.* Side chair. 1929–30. Solid hard maple frame with clear lacquer finish; webbed seat with cotton and hair filling. 17 x 19 x 37½". Adelta Oy

577.   *Black Villa.* Chair. 1908. Solid oak frame with decorated brass rods; padded mohair-covered seat and back. 24⅜ x 22 x 29⅞". Adelta Oy

578.   *Hannes.* Chair. 1908. Solid bent mahogany frame; foam-padded seat with crocodile cover. 22¹⁄₁₆ x 20½ x 36½". Adelta Oy

579.   *Saarinen House Lounge Chair.* Lounge chair. 1929–30. Solid hardwood frame; East Indian rosewood, African mahogany, Afrormosia, and maple veneers; clear lacquer finish. 33¾ x 30½ x 35½". Arkitektura

580.   *Saarinen House Armchair.* Armchair. 1929–30. Solid hardwood frame; East Indian rosewood, African mahogany, Afrormosia, and maple veneers; ebony trim; clear lacquer finish; black upholstery tacks. 24¾ x 21½ x 31". Adelta Oy

581.   *Saarinen House Credenza.* Credenza. 1929–30. Ply and solid hardwood frame; East Indian rosewood, African mahogany, Afrormosia, and maple veneers; ebony keyhole; brass hardware; clear lacquer finish; standard interior finish with four adjustable birch shelves with rosewood edging. 60 x 15 x 39½". Arkitektura

Alison and Peter Smithson (b. 1928 and 1923)

An extremely well designed building for the Hunstanton School in Norfolk, England (1924–54) and the famous Economist Building in London (1964) brought attention to this couple, whose questioning and controversial reflections have given new theoretical direction to a whole generation of English architects.

582.　Collector table. Silver lacquered wood with leather cushion; three lamps in option. 39⅜ x 39⅜ x 14¹³⁄₁₆″. Tecta Möbel

583.　*Waterlily and Fish*. Colored perspex-desk. Lacquered tubular steel. 39⅜ x 25⅞ x 28¾″. Tecta Möbel

Robert Stern (b. 1939)

A practicing architect whose buildings denote an eclectic and somewhat recherché combination of past and present architectural elements, Stern is also an architectural historian and critic and the talented author and host of the television series "Pride of Place: Building the American Dream." Professor at the Columbia University School of Architecture and head of the Temple Hoyne Buell Center for the Study of American Architecture, he received in 1985 the National Honor Award from the American Institute of Architects (AIA).

584.　*Century, Metropolitan, Harmonie*. Candlesticks. Silver-plated. Swid Powell

585.　*Majestic*. Plate. Diameter 12″. Swid Powell

Stanley Tigerman (b. 1930)

Trained at Yale and principal of the Chicago firm Tigerman Fugman McCurry, Tigerman was in 1980 appointed architect in residence at the American Academy in Rome. Twice chosen to show his works at the Venice Biennale, he is a controversial architect deeply concerned with American heritage and the Chicago style he has promoted through books and exhibitions. Tigerman's works and designs are widely published and have been exhibited at the Museum of Modern Art in New York.

586.　*Sunshine*. Plate. Diameter 12″. Swid Powell

587.　Coffeepot of five-piece coffee and tea service. Silver 925/1000; handles, spouts, and knobs in lost-wax casting. Alessi

Oscar Tusquets (b. 1941)

Co-founder of the Barcelona firm Studio PER and of B.D. Ediciones de Diseño, which produces items designed by Spanish architects as well as reeditions of furniture designs by Mackintosh and Gaudí, Tusquets is considered one of the best Spanish architects. His personal designs—private homes, extensions of the Barcelona School of Medicine, and Banco de España—were exhibited at the Museum of Modern Art in New York (1979), the London ICA (1983), the Paris Biennale (1985), and the Tokyo "Contemporary Design" exhibition of 1985.

588a–d.　Four-piece tea service. Teapot, sugar bowl, milk jug, tray. Silver 925/1000. Alessi

589.　Necklace. 18-kt. gold. Cleto Munari

Robert Venturi (b. 1925)

"I like elements that are hybrid rather than pure, compromising rather than clean, disturbed rather than straightforward," claimed the Philadelphia architect Venturi in his controversial book Complexity and Contradiction in Architecture, *which triggered many Post-Modern architectural movements.* Learning from Las Vegas *(1971), which he wrote with his wife, Denise Scott Brown, and Steven Izenour, advocates, similarly, the cultural value of American popular artifacts. Venturi's works—among them, North Pennsylvania Visiting Nurses Association Headquarters and Benjamin Franklin's house (Franklin Court), both in Philadelphia; the Vanna Venturi House in Chestnut Hill; Brandt-Johnson House in Colorado; and Wu Hall in Princeton—are unanimously considered to be contemporary American landmarks. Venturi's numerous and attractive projects in the United States and abroad all use subtle combinations of past formal references and vernacular patterns to express his decorative and ironic wit—and serve to illustrate his antimodernist statement "Less is a bore."*

590.　*Dashes*. Crystal glass set. Swid Powell

591.　Five-piece coffee and tea service. Teapot, sugar bowl, milk jug, coffeepot, "Campidoglio" tray. Silver 925/1000. Alessi

592.　*Cabriole Leg Table*. Table. Base in wood laminations faced with wood veneer or laminate; wooden square or round top with wood veneer or laminate or in solid granite. Square top 48″, 54″, or 60″; round top, diameter 54″ or 60″; height 28½″. Knoll International

593. *Queen Anne.* Chair. Frame in bentwood laminations faced with wood veneer or laminate, perforated with Queen Anne motif. 26¼ x 23½ x 38½". Knoll International

594. *Art Deco.* Chair. Frame in bentwood laminations faced with wood veneer or surf-white laminate with pattern hand-screened in epoxy inks; back perforated with Art Deco motif. 23½ x 23⅞ x 31¾". Knoll International

595. *Sheraton.* Chair. Frame in bentwood laminations faced with wood veneer or surf-white laminate with pattern applied on black laminate; back perforated with Sheraton motif. 23⅛ x 23⅞ x 33½". Knoll International

596. *Art Nouveau.* Chair. Frame in bentwood laminations faced with wood veneer or laminate, perforated with Art Nouveau motif. 23¼ x 23⅞ x 37½". Knoll International

597. *Gothic.* Chair. Frame in bentwood laminations faced with wood veneer or laminate, perforated with Gothic motif. 21½ x 23⅞ x 42". Knoll International

598. *Biedermeier.* Chair. Frame in bentwood laminations faced with wood veneer or laminate, perforated with Biedermeier motif. 23⅜ x 23⅞ x 34½". Knoll International

599. *Urn Table.* Table. Base in wood laminations faced with wood veneer or laminate, cut in urn motif; capped with zinc toes in black or polished chrome finish; round top in solid granite or with wood veneer or laminate with 1⅛"-wide natural maple edge. Diameter 54" or 60"; height 28½". Knoll International

600. Sofa. Frame in polyurethane foam over fiberglass and wooden deck; spring cushion support; cushions filled with foamed polyester batting. 87 x 43½ x 33¼". Knoll International

Frank Lloyd Wright (1867–1959)

The greatest of all American architects, Wright first worked as draftsman for the Chicago firm Adler and Sullivan (1888–93), where he became aware of Louis Sullivan's philosophy of organic growth and of the influence of the Arts and Crafts movement. His independent practice began in 1893 with the design of his own residence; he then built a series of magnificent houses in the suburbs of Chicago that later came to be known as the Prairie School, the climax of which was the Robie House (1907–9). At the same time, Wright designed the Larkin

Building in Buffalo, New York (1904, later destroyed), and the famous Oak Park Unity Church in Illinois (1905–7), both with structure, circulatory space, lighting, and ornamentation brilliantly interwoven to emphasize a clear, high central space. The Tokyo Imperial Hotel (1910) and the Chicago Midway Garden (1914, destroyed 1923), two projects in which he combined wit with heavy, decorative elements to manipulate public space, preluded a long period of isolation, little work, philosophical reflection, and growth of influence abroad. In 1921–23, Wright built the Millard House ("La Miniatura") in Pasadena, the most famous of several California houses he built out of decorated concrete blocks.

Fallingwater (1935–37), a cantilevered weekend home near Pittsburgh, and the Johnson Wax administration building in Racine, Wisconsin (1936–39), were two antagonist works designed not only to respond to the then spreading International Style but also to illustrate his Usonian philosophy. Wright, then in his seventies, began a second career, which culminated in the chapel of Florida Southern College (1940), the Unitarian Church in Madison, Wisconsin (1947), the Price Tower in Bartlesville, Oklahoma (1955), and the notorious Solomon R. Guggenheim Museum in New York City (1943–46, 1956–59), which he did not live to see completed.

601. Frieze panel. Plaster. 27 x 3 x 52". Heinz & Co.

602. *Midway 1.* Hexagonal-back chair. 1914. Cherrywood, natural or stained walnut, or black frame; seat and back foam-padded and upholstered with red, blue, or gray exclusive fabric or leather. 20¼ x 18⅞ x 34¼". Cassina

603. *Taliesen.* Armchair. 1949. Frame in laminated plywood veneered with cherrywood or natural or stained walnut; inner panels upholstered with polyurethane and polyester padding covered with red, blue, or gray exclusive fabric or leather. 37 x 35⅜ x 30⅓". Cassina

604. Floor lamp. Oak or mahogany. 10 x 14 x 65". Heinz & Co.

605. *Barrel.* Dining chair. 1937. Cherrywood or natural or stained walnut; seat in polyurethane foam covered with red, blue, or gray exclusive fabric or leather. 21½ x 21⅞ x 31⅞". Cassina

606. *Robie*. High-back chair. 1908. Natural cherrywood; polyurethane foam padding; upholstery in exclusive red, blue, or gray fabric or leather. 15¾ x 17⅞ x 53⅓". Cassina

607. *Allen*. Table. 1917. Natural cherrywood with staves top. 101⅜ x 41¾ x 27¾". Cassina

608. *Imperial Hotel Dinnerware*. 1922. Dinner plate, salad plate, bread and butter plate, soup bowl, salad bowl, cup and saucer. Heinz & Co.

609. *Midway 3*. Table. 1914. Base in glossy white, red, or gray enamelled steel; square or round crystal glass top; square table 47¼ x 47¼ x 27¾"; round table, diameter 47"; height 27¾". Cassina

610. *Midway 2*. Chair. 1914. Frame in glossy white, red, blue, or gray enamelled steel rod; seat and back padded with polyurethane foam covered with exclusive fabric. 15¾ x 18⅛ x 34⅝". Cassina

528

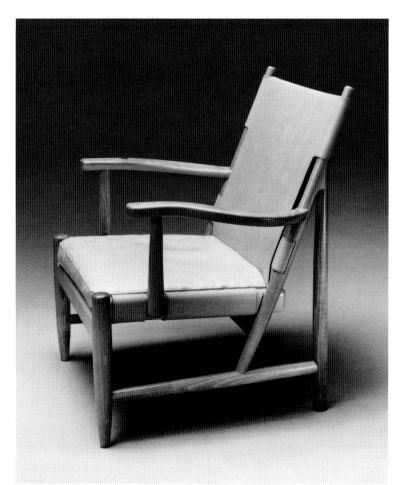

529

530

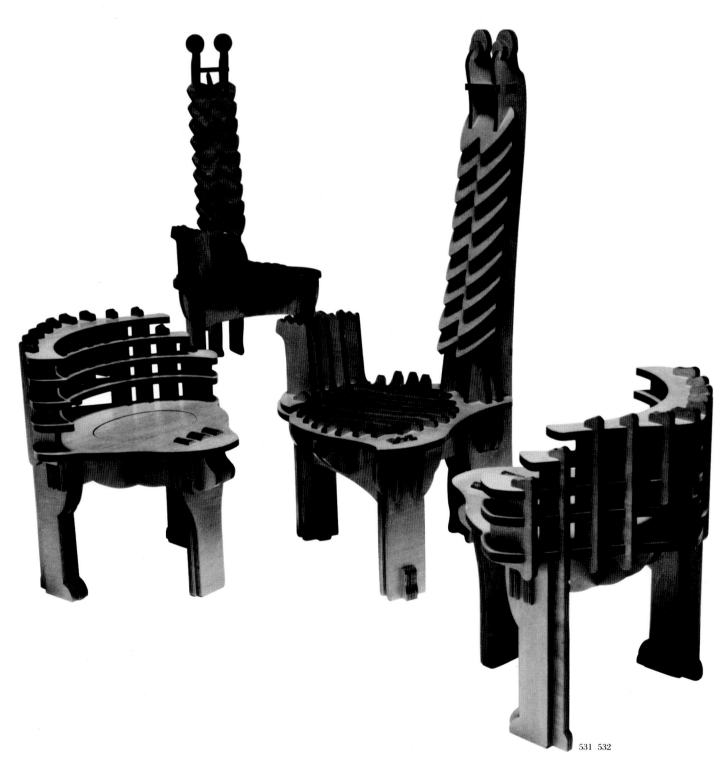

531 532

533

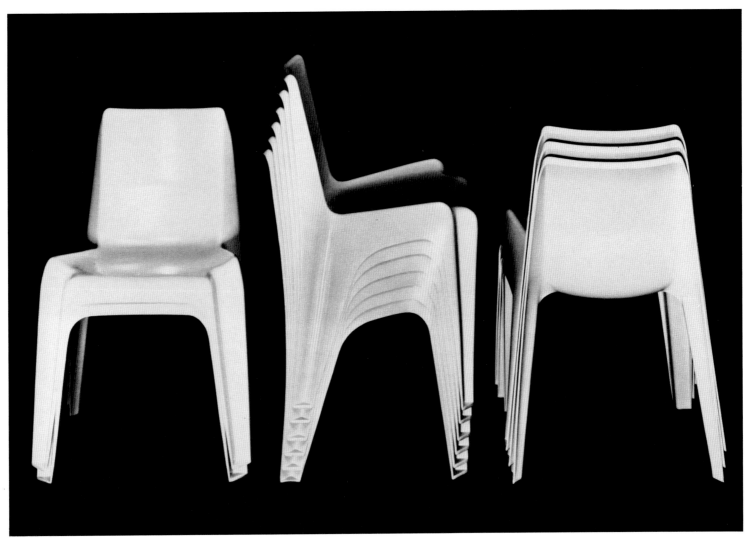

534

535

536

537

538

539 540

541

543

542

544

545

546

547

549

548

550

551

552

553

554

555

556

557

558

559 560

561

562

564

565 566

567

568

569

570

571

572

573

574

575

576

577

578

579

580

581

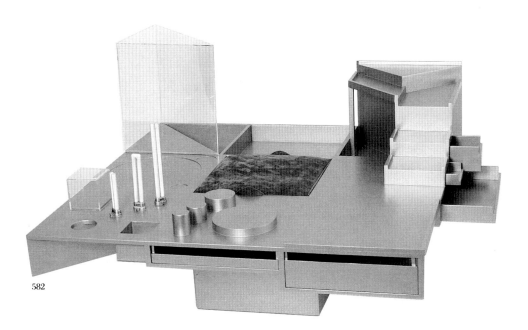

582

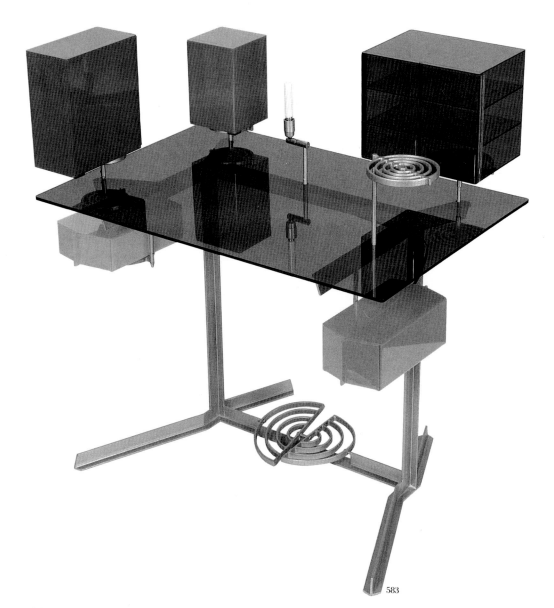

583

584

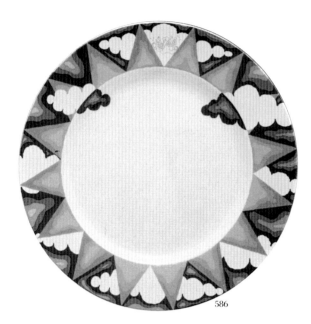

586

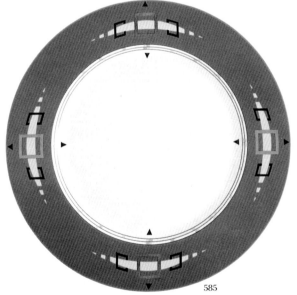

585

587

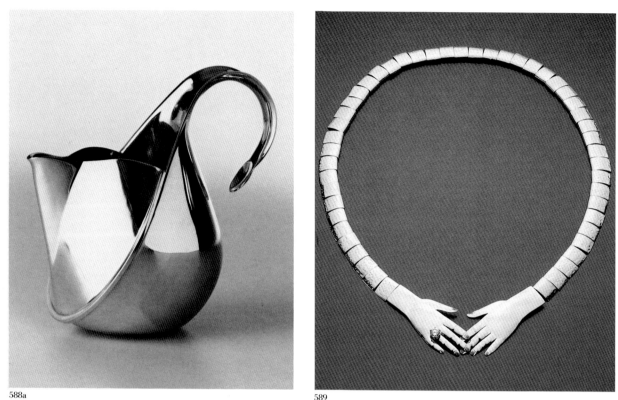

588a

589

588a–d

590

591

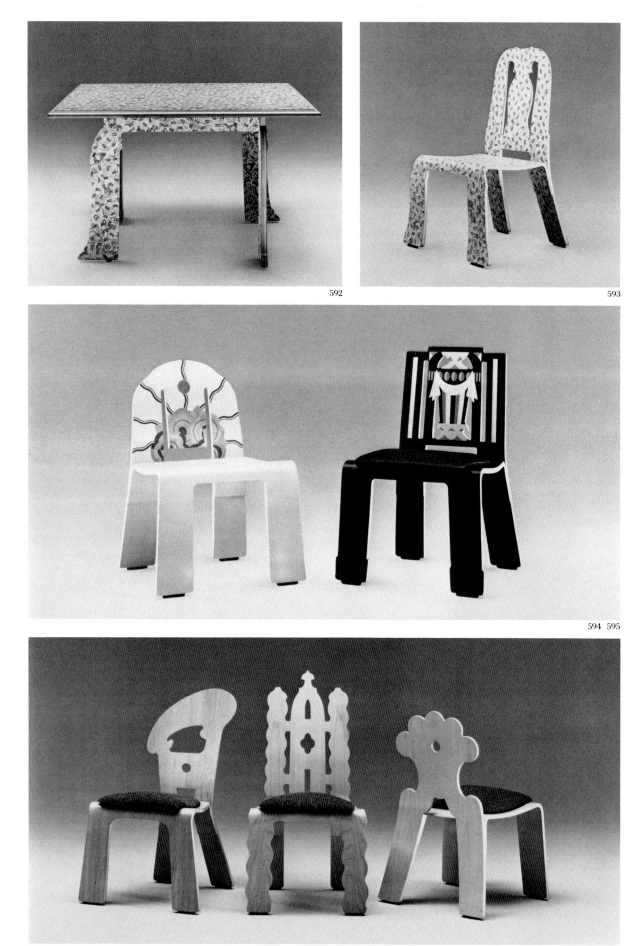

592

593

594 595

596–598

599

600

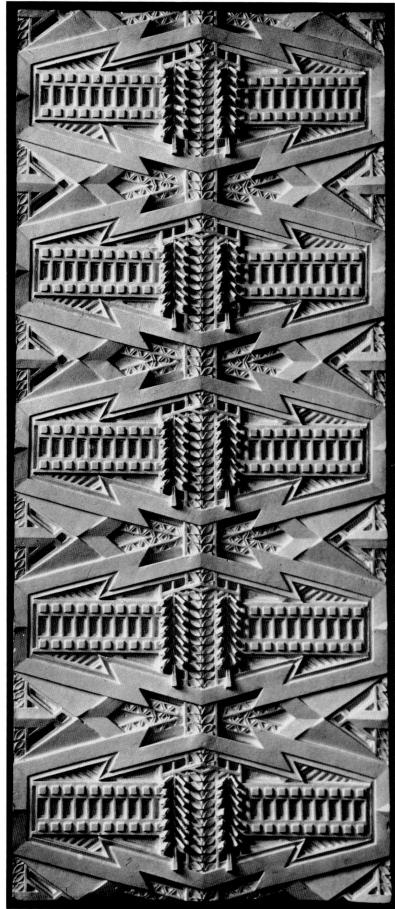

601

602

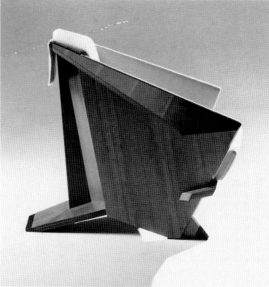

603

604

605

606 607

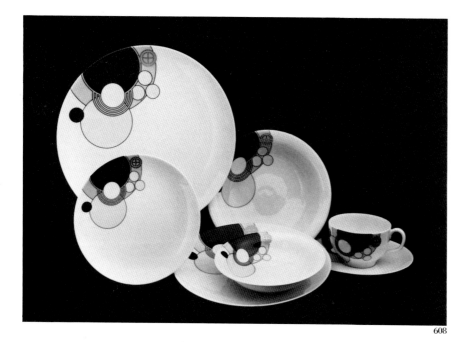

608

609

610

INDEX OF MANUFACTURERS

Note: The index below contains names and addresses for those manufacturers listed in the captions. A listing of American distributors for companies outside the United States is provided when this applies. Information regarding the furniture shown in this book may be obtained by writing the manufacturers and/or their distributors.

Adelta Oy
Tunturikatu 9A1
00100 Helsinki
Finland

Airborne
192, Boulevard Anatole France
93200 Saint-Denis
France

Alessi
Via Privata Alessi
28023 Crusinallo
Novara, Italy

U.S. Distributor
The Schwabel Corporation
281 Albany Street
Cambridge, Massachusetts 02139

Alias
Via Respighi, 2
20122 Milan
Italy

Apotem
Via Provinciale Est 15
S. Giovanni alla vena
56016 Pisa
Italy

Arkitektura
P.O. Box 210
Princeton, New Jersey 08540

Artek
Kēskúskatu 3
00100 Helsinki 10
Finland

U.S. Distributor
Scandinavian Design
127 East 59th Street
New York, New York 10022

Artemide
Via Burghiera
20010 Pregnana Milanese
Milan, Italy

U.S. Distributor
Artemide
150 East 58th Street
New York, New York 10155

Wiener Porzellanmanufactur Augarten
Schloss Augarten
Postfach 76
A-1021 Vienna II
Austria

Bachausen
Kärntnerstrasse 33
Postfach 81
A-1015 Vienna 1
Austria

B. D. Ediciones de Diseño
Mallorca 291
Barcelona 37
Spain

U.S. Distributor
Furniture of the Twentieth Century
227 West 17th Street
New York, New York 10011

Bermude
34, Rue Perier
92120 Montrouge
France

G.B. Bernini
Via Fiume 17
20048 Carate Brianza
Milan, Italy

André Bruyère Editions
7, Rue du Maine
75014 Paris
France

Candle
Via Salaino 7
20144 Milan
Italy

Casa Nova
62029 Tolentino
74500 Italy

Cassina
Via Luigi Busnelli 1
20036 Meda
Milan, Italy

U.S. Distributor
Atelier International
595 Madison Avenue
New York, New York 10022

Cheru Enterprises
2514 S. Grand Avenue
Los Angeles, California 90007

Cleto Munari
Piazzetta Ponte S. Paolo 1
36100 Vicenza
Italy

Cosanti Originals, Inc.
6433 Doubletree Road
Scottsdale, Arizona 85253

D S W
Rijkstraatweg 15
3300 A.N. Dordrecht
The Netherlands

Ecart International
111 Rue St. Antoine
75004 Paris
France

U.S. Distributor
Furniture of the Twentieth Century
227 West 17th Street
New York, New York 10011

Fontana Arte
Via Alzaia Trieste 49
20094 Corsico
Milan, Italy

Fusital
Via Gavazzi 16
22035 Canzol
Como, Italy

U.S. Distributor
Valli & Colom, Inc.
1540 Highland Avenue
Duarte, California 91010

Habit
Mülheimerstrasse 121a
5090, Leverkhusen
The Netherlands

Fritz Hansen
DK-3450, Allerød
Denmark

U.S. Distributor
ICF
305 East 63rd Street
New York, New York 10021

Heinz & Co.
P.O. Box 663
Oak Park, Illinois 60303

Hoekan
Matsubara 3–18–11
Setagaya-ku, Tokyo 156
Japan

Holzwerkstätten
Piaristengasse 24
A-1080 Vienna
Austria

U.S. Distributor
Designs, Inc.
232 East 59th Street
New York, New York 10022

ICF (Italy)
280 Strada Padana Superiore
20090 Vimodrone
Milan, Italy

ICF (U.S.)
305 East 63rd Street
New York, New York 10021

i4 Mariani
Via S. Antonio 102/104
22060 Perticato–Mariano Commense
Como, Italy

Images
San Marco 3159
30124 Venice
Italy

U.S. Distributor
Images of America
329 Blair Street
Thomasville, North Carolina 27360

Ittala Glassworks
14500 Ittala
Finland

U.S. Distributor
Ahlstrom Trading, Inc.
Ittala U.S.A.
175 Clearbrook Road
Elmsford, New York 10523

Le Klint
Egestubben 13-15
DK-5270 Odense N.
Denmark

Knoll International
The Knoll Building
655 Madison Avenue
New York, New York 10021

Kosuga & Co., Ltd.
Kosuga Building
15-4, 2-chome
Higashi-Nihonbashi, Chuo-ku
Tokyo, Japan

Larsen Furniture
41 East 11th Street
New York, New York 10003

J & L Lobmeyr
Kärntnerstrasse 26A
1015 Vienna
Austria

U.S. Distributor
J & L Lobmeyr
120 East 56th Street
New York, New York 10022

I.P. Lund
Axel Kiers Voj 9
DK-8270 Højbjerg
Denmark

Martinelli-Luce
Via Bandettini 155
55100 Lucca
Italy

A. Michelsen
Ragnade 7
2100 Copenhagen
Denmark

Herman Miller
8500 Byron Road
Zeeland, Michigan 49464

Mira-X
Internationale Textilverlag
CH-5034 Suhr
Switzerland

U.S. Distributor
Mira-X International Furnishing
246 East 58th Street
New York, New York 10022

Misura Emme
Via IV Novembre 72
22066 Mariano Commense
Como, Italy

Möbel Industrie Design
Assmayergasse 60/24
A-1120 Vienna
Austria

Mobilier International
162, Boulevard Voltaire
75011 Paris
France

Molteni & Co.
Via Rossini
20034 Giussano
Italy

Nikol Internazionale, Delta Export
Via Palladio 23
Zona Industriale
33010 Tavagnacco Udine
Italy

Olivari
Via G. Matteotti 140
28021 Borgomanero
Novara, Italy

Poltronova
Via Provinciale Pratese 23
51037 Montale
Pistoia, Italy

Louis Poulsen
A/S Nyhavn 11
DK-1004 Copenhagen
Denmark

U.S. Distributor
Scan Furniture
Greenbelt Consumer Services, Inc.
Greenwood Place
Savage, Maryland 20863

Rosenthal Aktiengesellschaft
Postfach 1520
8672, Selb/Bayern
Federal Republic of Germany

Rossi & Arcandi
Via Brenta 4
36010, Moticello Conte Otto
Vicenza, Italy

Salzburger Cristallglass
Adolf-Schemelstrasse 11–13
Postfach 11
A-5033 Salzburg
Austria

Schlapp-Möbel
Postfach 69
D-6392 New Anspach 1
Federal Republic of Germany

Sentou
12, Rue des Francs Bourgeois
75003 Paris
France

Skipper Italy
Via S. Spirito 14
20121 Milan
Italy

U.S. Distributors
Abitare
212 East 57th Street
New York, New York 10022

Fortree, Inc.
8801 Beverly Boulevard
Los Angeles, California 90048

La Verne Galleries
3925 N. Miami Avenue
Miami, Florida 33137

Thomas Design
2941 Hennepin Avenue
Minneapolis, Minnesota 55408

Rubinetterie Stella
Via Unitá d'Italia, 1
28100 Novara
Italy

A/S Stelton
10, Grusbakken, DK-2820, Gentofte
P.O. Box 23
Copenhagen, Denmark

Stilnovo
Via F. Ferruccio 8
20145 Milan
Italy

Sunar
18, Marshall Street
Norwalk, Ottawa 06854
Canada

SunarHauserman
5711 Grant Avenue
Cleveland, Ohio 44105

Svenskt Tenn
Stradvägen 5
11451 Stockholm
Sweden

Swid Powell
55 East 57th Street
New York, New York 10022

Tecno
Via Bigli 22
20121 Milan
Italy

Tecta Möbel
Sohnreystrasse 18
3471 Lauenförde
Federal Republic of Germany

Tendo Brasileira
Av. Independencia 3200
Loteamento Industrial
Taubaté
Cep 12100
Est. São Paulo
Brazil

Thonet
491 East Prince Street
P.O. Box 1587
York, Pennsylvania 17405

Gebrüder Thonet
Michael-Thonetstrasse 1
3558 Frankenberg
Federal Republic of Germany

USM
CH-3110 Münsingen
Switzerland

Venini
Fondamente Vetrai
Murano Venice
Italy

Vereinigte Werkstätten für Kunst im Handwerk AG
Ridlerstrasse 31
8000 Munich
Federal Republic of Germany

Franz Wittmann
A-3492, Etsdorf am Kamp
Austria

Woka-Beleuchtungskörper
Singerstrasse 16
A-1010 Vienna
Austria

U.S. Distributor
George Kovacs, Inc.
831 Madison Avenue
New York, New York 10021

Zanotta
Via Vittorio Veneto 57
20054 Nova Milanese
Italy

U.S. Distributor
ICF
305 East 63rd Street
New York, New York 10021

ACKNOWLEDGMENTS

This book originated from the simple idea that if architects design projects they sometimes build, then they also design furniture and objects, the latter a subject I felt would be interesting to pursue. The field of investigation turned out to be far broader than assumed. Some of the items are still produced or are being issued as re-editions by famous manufacturers. The rest had to be found and identified through a compilation of numerous furniture catalogues and trade magazines. The quest was long, but through it all I received the constant help and invaluable support of my wife, Vica, and my agent, Phyllis Wender. Thanks must also go to Joan Kron, who offered guidance at the initial stages, and to Paul Gottlieb, Margaret Kaplan, Anne Yarowsky, the late Patrick Cunningham, Margaret Rennolds, and Gilda Hannah at Harry N. Abrams, Inc.

—M. E.